What people are saying about …

Soul Custody

"*Soul Custody* is a clarion call—a prophetic call to do something significant with your life before it's too late. This book points the way to real life as God intended. No one is better qualified to write on this topic than Stephen W. Smith. I highly recommend it."

Gary Chapman, PhD, author of *The Five*
Love Languages and *Love as a Way of Life*

"The God who redeemed our souls has given us the responsibility to become custodians of their care. Our souls are constantly under siege by the culture; they need to be restored and nurtured. But sadly, most of us take better care of our cars than our souls! Stephen W. Smith has listened to the Word and to his own needy soul, and though he confesses he has come late to the process, he provides priceless counsel for taking custody of our own souls."

Michael Card, author and musician

"A great, refreshing read! *Soul Custody* gives us the permission to live intentional lives, in which we let God care for us even as we care for others. I wish I'd had it in my hands years ago. Motivating, thoughtful, really doable, this book could set you on the life course you really long for."

Paula Rinehart, author of *Strong Women,*
Soft Hearts and *Better Than My Dreams*

"*Soul Custody* is more than a book title—it's a clear, specific, and direct appeal for us to care for the part of us that's most lasting and real. With strong yet gentle guidance, Steve shows us how to make soul-caring choices, anchored in the vastness of God's limitless love, that will provide strength, direction, and equilibrium to every other aspect of our lives. This is a *must*-read for anyone convinced that there's nothing worth more than their soul."

Fil Anderson, author of *Running on Empty* and *Breaking the Rules*

"*Soul Custody* is filled with powerful invitations that will encourage your pursuit of an abundant life in Christ. Steve Smith brings to life the many benefits of soul guardianship and offers practical suggestions that are within-reach realities for all who hunger for a deeper faith journey … not just for the holier-than-normal soul-care experts!"

Stephen A. Macchia, DMin, founder and president, Leadership Transformations, Inc., and author of *Becoming a Healthy Church*

"I am very enthusiastic about Stephen W. Smith's latest book, *Soul Custody.* I am grateful that he has given many years to get in touch with the souls of so many by walking with them compassionately and listening to them well. He sounds an alarm and makes a passionate, persuasive appeal to us about the forces in our contemporary culture that war against the health of our souls and, therefore, of our whole being. From this experience, gained firsthand in his life and through that of many others, he also has learned the ways we need to become proactive in caring for our souls, that we might become the persons God created us and Christ redeemed us to be. I heartily recommend this book, both for individual use and for use in groups of those who want to walk and work together to care for the health of their souls. Thank you, Steve, for giving us this fruit of your life and ministry!"

Douglas Stewart, director of spiritual formation, InterVarsity Christian Fellowship

"Stephen W. Smith has written a book that we need. Amidst the noise of Twitter, Facebook, reality television, and our drive for muchness, *Soul Custody* calls us to a daily union with God that actually seems reachable. The good, good news that God longs for our presence and is always present for us is the message that can set us free!"

Sharon A. Hersh, MA, licensed professional counselor and author of *Bravehearts*, *The Last Addiction*, and *Begin Again, Believe Again*

"Steve Smith knows what he's talking about when he writes of *Soul Custody*. For many years, the ministry he and his wife lead, Potter's Inn, has helped people care for their soul. There are few things more important than Christians, especially those who are leaders, caring for their soul in the constant battle against burnout. This book can enhance your spiritual health."

Bryant Wright, senior pastor, Johnson Ferry Baptist Church, Marietta, GA

"*Soul Custody* gave me hope for my relationship with God. Steve reminded me that I get to make choices that take me closer to God.

I not only get to make those decisions, but I already am. And *Soul Custody* helped me to see and think through so many of them. Maybe things really can change in my relationship with Him."

Palmer Trice, director,
The Barnabas Center, Charlotte, NC

"We live in a world where most of us react and let life happen to us. Stephen W. Smith, in his book *Soul Custody,* makes us take hold of our lives and stop making excuses. Powerful and painfully pointed, it reaches to the heart. It reached to my heart."

Jim Kallam, senior pastor,
Church of Charlotte, Charlotte, NC

"A must-read for worn-out Christians, *Soul Custody* provides the critical bridge between boundaries and the Beatitudes. Building upon a solid foundation of Scripture and church history, the reader receives not only a blueprint for the spiritual life, but the tools to get building."

Rev. Sara Singleton, pastor of spiritual formation,
First Presbyterian Church, Colorado Springs, CO

"*Soul Custody* will show you how to diagnose the state of your own soul and make some midcourse corrections. It is about learning how to live your life a different way, a with-God way. It is written with care, creativity, and the authority of experience."

Gary W. Moon, PhD, vice president and chair
of integration, Richmont Graduate University,
and author of *Apprenticeship with Jesus*

Soul
Custody

Soul
Custody

CHOOSING TO CARE FOR THE
ONE AND ONLY YOU

STEPHEN W. SMITH

David C Cook®

transforming lives together

SOUL CUSTODY
Published by David C Cook
4050 Lee Vance View
Colorado Springs, CO 80918 U.S.A.

David C Cook Distribution Canada
55 Woodslee Avenue, Paris, Ontario, Canada N3L 3E5

David C Cook U.K., Kingsway Communications
Eastbourne, East Sussex BN23 6NT, England

The graphic circle C logo is a registered trademark of David C Cook.

All Scripture quotations, unless otherwise noted, are taken from the *Holy Bible,
New International Version*. *NIV.* Copyright © 1973, 1978, 1984 by International
Bible Society. Used by permission of Zondervan. All rights reserved. Scripture
quotations marked MSG are taken from *THE MESSAGE.* Copyright © by Eugene
H. Peterson 1993, 1994, 1995, 1996, 2000, 2001, 2002. Used by permission of
NavPress Publishing Group. Scripture quotations marked NLT are taken from the
New Living Translation of the Holy Bible. New Living Translation copyright ©
1996, 2004 by Tyndale Charitable Trust. Used by permission of Tyndale House
Publishers. Scripture quotations marked ESV are taken from *The Holy Bible, English
Standard Version.* Copyright © 2000; 2001 by Crossway Bibles, a division of Good
News Publishers. Used by permission. All rights reserved. Scripture quotations
marked NKJV are taken from the New King James Version. Copyright © 1982 by
Thomas Nelson, Inc. Used by permission. All rights reserved. Scripture quotations
marked KJV are taken from the King James Version of the Bible. (Public Domain.)
Scripture quotations marked AB are taken from *The Amplified Bible.* Copyright
© 1954, 1958, 1962, 1964, 1965, 1987 by The Lockman Foundation. Used by
permission. The author has added italics to some Scripture quotations for emphasis.

LCCN 2010928037
ISBN 978-1-4347-6472-0
eISBN 978-0-7814-0506-5

© 2010 Stephen W. Smith

The Team: John Blase, Sarah Schultz, Erin Prater, Karen Athen
Cover Design: Amy Kiechlin

Printed in the United States of America
First Edition 2010

2 3 4 5 6 7 8 9 10

042214

Dedication

This book is dedicated to the men and women who support the Potter's Inn, a Christian ministry devoted to spiritual formation and the care of the soul. I stand on your shoulders, and you are the real foundation of everything we do, say, write, and offer! Thank you for walking into the initial risk and chaos with us as we sought to live out a dream, follow a vision, and offer our hearts to others on the journey. You have helped me take custody of my own soul by investing your love and resources into the ministry of Potter's Inn. The effects of your love and support now extend throughout the world via this book.

With profound gratitude and all blessings,
Stephen W. Smith
Potter's Inn
www.pottersinn.com

Contents

Acknowledgments

C. S. Lewis told us, "We read to know that we are not alone." But when we write, it can sometimes feel very lonely. What is true is that many voices have spoken into this book over the years. This book may best be described as a volume of collective voices who have tried all the time, failed some of the time, and sometimes succeeded in taking custody of their own souls in the midst of turmoil, chaos, and opportunity. I hope it will be a helpful resource for you in your own journey.

These voices and souls have stood out to me and helped form the words when I did not know how to find them. My heartfelt thanks to Steve Forney, John and Denise Kapitan, David Sachsenmaier, Donovan Graham, Gloria Schwartz, Chuck and Kim Millsap, Russell and Kate Courtney, and Rebekah Ormord, my assistant, for loving me and caring for the themes of this book in significant ways.

I want to thank the David C. Cook team for embracing this book and the need for it—and for shouldering it with me in every step! I love being a part of this publishing family, which is so creative, bold, and transforming. My editor, John Blase, is my companion in these themes. John, you have been extraordinarily patient and kind, and I have needed both patience and kindness. I like the way we work together! Eric and Elisa Stanford stepped into the chapters early on and helped me develop, shape, and transform my early thoughts into better thinking than I could do alone. Don Pape has become a cheerleader for this message and me, and for that I'm grateful. Amy Kiechlin captured my message via the cover, and I'm so very grateful for her artistic gifts! Kathy Helmers is my literary agent and companion on this publishing adventure. Thank you, Kathy, for your coaching and encouraging words!

No voice, no soul, no person can ever match that of my lifelong companion and wife, Gwen. We've carved out these words together, though it's my name on the cover. I'm forever grateful and glad to call you my soul friend, spiritual director, and lover all in one soul. You are my *anam cara!* I am the most fortunate of all.

1

Soul Care

Healing the Violence Done to Your Soul

There is a way that seems right to a
man, but in the end it leads to death.
—*Proverbs 14:12*

The violence done us by others
is often less painful than that
which we do to ourselves.
—*François de La Rochefoucauld*

We're in trouble. We need help. The American dream has turned into
an all-too-real nightmare that sears our minds as we try to sleep. Life
is not working as we think it should.

Look around you. Listen. You can feel it.

It's the violence.

News updates constantly inform us that our world is in trouble.
Rates of domestic violence are up; gang violence is out of control in
many communities; rates of sexual abuse against children are on the
rise; substance and prescription drug abuse are rampant. We dead-
bolt our doors at night and sleep with security alarms set because we

fear the violence, the possible harm. We're convinced it is crouching at our door.

Job-loss reports and economic peril have acted like napalm, vaporizing our dreams of a retired life on a sunny beach. I recently asked fifty business leaders, "How many of you in this room are living with more fear today than at any other time in your life?" Every single one of them raised a hand.

Technology has been both a blessing and a curse. For some of us, life has no meaning apart from Twitter and the Internet. We feel enslaved by our laptops and can't get along without them. Google brings instant information, but little inspiration. We are overwhelmed at the e-mails, voice mails—even the snail mail crammed into our physical mailboxes.

Uncertainty plagues our lives. Talk shows spin pseudo-optimism, and we momentarily believe that maybe it's not all that bad. Deep down, though, we know it is.

And it is the deep down that concerns me most. We can't sleep. We don't eat right. We're constantly on the go, burning the candle at both ends. Is it any wonder that eight of the top ten drugs prescribed by doctors are mood-altering substances to help us cope with our interior turmoil?

We are sowing havoc and reaping the whirlwind. We are giving up ground that should never be surrendered. We are doing more but living less, making a living but not having a life. Some days it feels like nothing more than rearranging the deck chairs on the sinking *Titanic* of our lives.

Violence, all of it. It may not all be physical violence, but it's still destructive to us and the lives we'd like to live. The outer violence of the world rushes in and does its work on the inside, deep down in our souls.

Look inside. Do you see evidence of soul violence going on in there?

You don't have to answer me. I know you do. So do I.

We need help. Our very lives are in jeopardy. Is this hell on earth the only way to live until we die? Annie Dillard, a writer, stops us in our tracks: "How we spend our days is, of course, how we spend our lives." If Dillard is right (and I believe she is), redeeming the day is more than just a slogan. We need our days to improve so that our lives can improve.

Can't we be saved from more than just our sins?

The wonderful news is that this salvation does exist. God never intended for us to suffer the kind of violence that's being inflicted upon us. He never intended for us to inflict more violence upon ourselves through our own poor decision making. God provides means for us to be healed from the damage done. The kinds of choices we must make to find healing and experience transformation fall under the umbrella of soul care.

I like to remember that the word *care* has its roots in a Latin word that means "cure." As we learn to care for our souls, we will also find a sense of healing from the violence happening in and around us. Caring and curing go together.

Thomas Merton said, "To allow oneself to be carried away by a multitude of conflicting concerns, to surrender to too many demands, to commit oneself to too many projects, to want to help everyone in everything is to succumb to violence." The choice is really not difficult to comprehend. We can either choose to succumb to the outer and inner violence that we are now living in or choose to live in a different way—right here and right now.

We can choose to care for our souls.

The Healing Way

Every single person who feels more dead than alive, more tired than energized, more burned-out than motivated, more unfulfilled than thriving is a soul in need—a soul who needs to be cared for. The Chinese have two characters for the English word *busyness,* which they define as "heart annihilation." We're killing ourselves with all of our busy, busy, busy. One of the reasons for the overwhelming amount of annihilation around us and in us is that the sin of busyness is very subtle. It's a subtle sin because busyness is validated, applauded, and affirmed everywhere—and sometimes especially among Christians.

A busy marketplace leader came to me for help, saying he was coming unglued due to all the stress in his life. He began our conversation this way: "Steve, I have a lawyer to keep me legal. I have a doctor to keep me healthy. I have a tax guy to keep me solvent. But I have no one to care for my soul. I feel like I'm going down."

I went through a long season during which my own life was being annihilated. I was affirmed for my hard work, and the evidence around me validated my strong work ethic. I attacked each day as something to be conquered. I did more, worked harder, and accomplished a lot in my career. But I was coming up empty inside. The carnage around me was growing. I was losing my soul even though I was gaining the world. Little by little my soul was eroding inside me. My marriage went south. My relationship with my four young sons—well, it was more like I sprinkled "father dust" on them during my quick appearances at meals and, occasionally, at bedtime. Yet I was being affirmed for my successes. Something was deadly wrong. I paid the great price of nearly losing all to gain what, in the end, doesn't matter at all.[1]

The purpose of *Soul Custody* is to help you take back what you might have lost along the way while living your life. Why should we lose our lives in vain attempts to live? For me, caring for my soul has been a journey to reclaim my life—the life I want to live and the life I was intended to live. By choosing to live in life-giving ways, my own life is being healed, cured, restored. Yours can be too!

Soul Custody

Taking custody of your own soul is all about being mindful of your soul and your God, your life and your future, your heart and what it's beating for—whether for the sacred or only for what is of this world. Being mindful of your soul simply requires loving the Lord your God with all of your heart and mind. Sometimes loving God is easier than mindfully choosing to live in ways that are life-giving—not heart annihilating.

Soul custody is taking back what we've almost lost in order to gain what we should never want to lose. It's doing what the word *custody* implies—taking responsibility for our souls and hearts. This is our sacred privilege.

Of course we really share joint custody of our souls with God. But we can be sure that He will do His part to look after our souls' well-being. Are we holding up our end of the partnership?

Abdicating our role as the custodian of our own souls is handing over our responsibility to someone or something else who may not have our best interests in mind. You know as well as I that there is always someone who wants to tell us how to live, what to buy, where to go. Relinquishing the God-given role of caring for our souls usually results in the paying of a tremendous price, not once, but throughout life. We can choose to sit down and throw our hands up in surrender, or we can assume the God-given role each of us has in caring for our souls. The choice is ours to make.

For example, if we allow our culture to be our soul's guardian, we will find ourselves in a continual game of tug-of-war in which we feel pulled between what we're told to do and what we ought to do. If, on the other hand, we step up to our responsibility to care for our own souls, we can begin to see the transformation that our hearts have secretly yearned for all along. This really is possible—believers through the ages have practiced and benefited from soul care.

As you know, we are not the first to feel the threat for our lives. What we are missing are the old, trusted lessons given us by wise sages, courageous prophets, desert fathers and mothers who knew some things that we need to discover for ourselves—before it's too late. They, like us, made choices about how they would deal with their own plights—natural disasters, governments gone astray, eras in which disease wiped out entire generations and wars were fought in their own backyards.

What we are going to learn in *Soul Custody* is how to find our way back to some of those old ways.

The Old Ways

Hundreds of years before Jesus was even born, a Jewish prophet stood in the face of his own culture's demise and said,

Ask for the ancient paths,
Where the good way is, and walk in it;
And you will find rest for your souls. (Jer. 6:16 NASB)

The old ways we will explore in this book have been time-tested and documented by men and women who throughout the centuries lived out these choices in their own lives and for their own souls' sake. They used these ways and choices to help them outlast the whitewater rapids of life that people have navigated for centuries. And in the process they found the life Jesus has wanted for us since the beginning—a life that is rich and satisfying. This is "real and eternal life, more and better life than they ever dreamed of" (John 10:10 MSG). Collectively, these courageous souls warned people of the doom ahead unless a different path was chosen. Today we need to hear that prophetic voice again before it's too late—before we lose custody of our own souls.

Listen to how Eugene Peterson renders it: "Many people think that what's written in the Bible has mostly to do with getting people into heaven—getting right with God and saving their eternal souls. It does have to do with that, of course, but not mostly. It is equally concerned with living on this earth—living well and living in a robust sanity."[2]

We each have only one soul. We will not get another. This is the only life we will live—so let's live it well! In living life well, we honor God, honor every facet of our souls, and see that the life that Jesus offers us really is a life of "robust sanity." Soul care is living with the end in mind but also living well now.

I wonder if you noticed the subtitle on the cover of this book. I don't want you to miss it: "Choosing to Care for the One and

Only You." You will not be given another life. Or, as you've probably
heard, *this is no dress rehearsal.* This is it. You have already begun the
journey. You may be just getting started or possibly having to rethink
everything due to a crisis, threat, or tragedy. It doesn't matter where
you are. You can begin to live a better, different life.

There are regrets in my life. One is simply this: I wish I would
have known then what I know now. Had I known these ways, these
practices, I believe I could have made better decisions about how to
live my life. At least that's what I believe today! So much impacts our
one and only life, body, and soul. I wish someone had written this
book earlier.

I am going to give you the chance to diagnose the state of your
own soul and hopefully make some important corrections. Together
we'll explore ways that seem right but aren't, choices some thought
would bring life but brought nothing but the stench of death. These
people are best described as the living dead … barely. As I've sat with
thousands of men and women who all are wanting the same thing—
life—I have seen how so many have made tragic choices that have only
led to lives filled with regret and pain.

No matter where you are on life's spectrum, it's time right now
to start living. It's time to take custody of your one and only soul.

In Defense of Soul Care

As I talk to people about soul care, I sometimes get resistance. It often
sounds like this: "Steve, doesn't the message of soul care contradict
some of the most fundamental teachings of Jesus Christ, like, 'Deny
yourself,' and, 'The man who hates his life will keep it'?"

I suppose the people who object in this way are just trying to be faithful to the Scriptures. But please hear me on this: Caring for your soul is never a selfish or egotistical act. In fact, caring for your soul is the opposite of being narcissistic. It is really an act of stewardship. We steward our souls by caring for them well. How can we continually give what we do not have? Caring for the soul is an act through which God can replenish your heart, restore your soul, and revive your day so you can meet the challenges of life, work, and relationships. Far from being labeled as sin, soul care is actually a biblical command.

- Proverbs 4:23: "Above all else, guard your heart. For it is the wellspring of life."
- Deuteronomy 4:9 (ESV): "Only take care, and keep your soul diligently."
- 1 Timothy 4:16: "Watch your life and doctrine closely."

As I view today's Christian landscape, there are many more programs, seminars, and strategies on this and that. But seldom are we encouraged to watch out for—and take custody of—our souls.

But perhaps most telling is the way Scripture links loving ourselves and loving others.

We first see this in Leviticus 19:18. It's given as an actual law. Here we read, "Love your neighbor as yourself. I am the LORD." Obviously this assumes that we love ourselves. And to love ourselves means to take care of ourselves, body and soul.

Other biblical writers expound on this necessary principle multiple times. Jesus Himself says loving God and loving our neighbors as ourselves are the greatest of all the commandments in the entire law (Matt. 22:37–40). Paul repeated that loving our neighbors as ourselves is the summation of the commandments (Rom. 13:9). James calls this kind of love the "royal law" (James 2:8).

When we love ourselves in a healthy way, we are actually moving away from self-centeredness and selfishness, not toward them. True love breeds life. It does not kill life. Paul reminds us that love "does not demand its own way" (1 Cor. 13:5 NLT).

It is not God who looks down on taking care of oneself. It is our culture that is guilty of spinning the idea of loving ourselves to be self-ish. As Walter Trobisch reminds us, "Indeed, we are so ingrained with the idea of self-denial, self-sacrifice, and the fear of being egotistical that the admonition to love one's self seems almost a blasphemy."[3]

And remember, we are not *just* caring for ourselves when we practice our own soul care. We are caring for every single person, thing, event, or aspect of our lives that we will touch and influence. As Bill, a lawyer for a national law practice, confided in me: "Steve, if I go down, I'll take a lot of people with me. I cast a big shadow whether I like it or not. I've got to get a grip on what is happening in me and around me."

That's what is so painful about an imploding soul. Initially it's a very private feeling, but the ripple effect of one person imploding can have dire consequences for those closest to him or her: the spouse, children, colleagues, and more. When a leader goes down, many people are affected for a very long time. When a man has an affair, when a woman suffers from abuse, or when a child is not loved, it is catastrophic. This is why caring for our souls is so strategic and important. But the opposite is also true: When the values of caring for the soul are embraced, the ripple effect is life-giving and God honoring.

We find again and again that it becomes difficult to love others well when there is no love and care for ourselves. So if you are worried that soul care might be selfish, please give that up.

The flight attendants on most airlines says it well: "In the unlikely event of cabin depressurization, place the oxygen mask first on yourself; then help the person or child next to you." You can't help anyone else if you are dying for lack of oxygen. It is not a selfish act for you to breathe first, then help the others in need. I hope you agree with me on that.

But now we need to consider what we really mean when we talk about our souls. After all, how do we care for what most of us really don't understand?

Understanding the Soul

The American poet Mary Oliver was right when she said, "No one knows what the soul is." Wise men and women in every culture, religion, and time have tried to explain it. There are Hebrew, Greek, Latin, and French words to help us. But if you look for a simple, easy-to-understand definition of the soul, you'll be hard-pressed to find one. The soul has remained a slippery, elusive topic subject to debate. For some, it's even scary. Some even think it is New Age-ish to speak of the soul.

Yet as far back as history has been recorded, there have been men and women who have spoken of the life within. Call it *soul, spirit, heart, will,* or something else—we still need to grasp what it is we need to take care of in this life.

At the beginning of the twenty-first century, we are learning much about the human body. We are making great advances in the war against cancer. We have figured out the structure of DNA and can discern our genetic roots. Stem cell research is all the rage. Yet knowing our souls—understanding the most important part of a human being—is a topic that's sadly neglected. No surgeon's knife can find the soul within us. It's not hiding behind our hearts or just below our kidneys.

D. H. Lawrence wrote, "I am not a mechanism, an assembly of various sections." I believe Lawrence was right. None of us is a machine, built to be wound up, jump started, or given a tune-up to run again until we finally wear out. We are far more complicated than that.

When we were conceived, not only were fearful and wonderful bodies formed, fearful and wonderful souls were made. Job reminds us of our beginnings when he says,

> *Oh, that marvel of conception as you stirred together*
> *semen and ovum—*
> *What a miracle of skin and bone,*
> *muscle and brain!*
> *You gave me life itself, and incredible love.*
> *You watched and guarded every breath I took. (Job*
> *10:10–12 MSG)*

This "marvel of conception" that Job told us about matters. Your soul is this marvelous and sacred life within you. When you look at your spouse, your children, your friends, you are looking at souls—souls who need just what you need. Everything that is alive needs some form of care. No living thing can survive, much less thrive, without being replenished with life-giving sustenance. You are not the exception. Every living thing needs care.

Our souls and bodies were God made, not manufactured. We are not machines. We are soulful beings. When God created the first human being, the first breath given to the man made from dirt gave him his soul. We read, "God formed Man out of dirt from the ground and blew into his nostrils the breath of life. The Man came alive—a living soul!" (Gen. 2:7 MSG). From Adam through you and I—we are living souls!

In short, your soul is the real you, the whole shebang—your heart, mind, emotions, desires, and longings all make up your soul. Look in the mirror and you will see more than your body—you will glimpse your soul. The life that is within you is your living soul. It is the truest part of you, and it will live on after you die.

Your soul is the real you. Your body is just the outerwear you live in while on Earth. You may prefer different outerwear, as many of us do. I'd like more hair and have never really understood why my body is hair impaired. But there's nothing impaired about my soul or yours in terms of the way they were made.

The real you, which God envisioned when He first had you in mind, is deeply loved and is a reflection of God's image. Your soul is God given, God shaped, God sustained. Yet, as we will find, we play a vital and necessary role in our own soul care. The real and the only you—that part of yourself that is alive right now as you are reading this book—is what matters the most. Take care of you.

Taking Custody of Your Soul

Soul care has incredible potential for good that goes beyond what we might expect. It has benefits for us, benefits for others, and even— believe it or not—benefits for God. These are the benefits that God wants us to take hold of by embracing soul care.

As we care for the soul within us, our lives are transformed in many ways. We will enjoy vast benefits like:

- peace and serenity, even in the midst of trying times.
- an exuberance about life and an ability to enjoy it.
- an ability to make soulful connections with friends.
- a growing awareness of God and intimate relationship with Him.
- fulfillment through our work and participation in something greater than just "doing our jobs."

But soul care is not just about focusing on ourselves. It is a very active and involved life. As we care for our own souls, we will inevitably become more aware of the dire conditions of the souls around us. We will sense need. We will want to help. We can help to change the situation. But not if we are empty—not if we are depleted and burned-out. The poet David Whyte speaks truth: "When your eyes are tired the world is tired also."

The real benefit of taking custody of our souls is that we honor God in caring for what He most cares for—us! When we live in healthy ways, we protect our souls from living in continual violence—we are living the "rich and satisfying" life Jesus spoke about and promised—the life He lived!

For example, when we choose to observe the Sabbath, we spend time truly present with God. He is glorified when we take up work that is truly His calling for us, work that fulfills His will. And He is glorified when we care for our bodies and value them as His created "marvel."

These are just some of the benefits we can create if we embrace soul care.

And they are the benefits we forfeit if we continue in the way we are going.

One day Jesus issued a prophetic cry that, if anything, echoes louder today in our overstimulated world. He said, "What good will it be for a man if he gains the whole world, yet forfeits his soul?" (Matt. 16:26). Jesus knew that life is more than doing stuff and accumulating things. Amid all of our gaining, we also need to understand what we are losing: our very souls.

You and I have a clear and high probability of losing our souls while trying to live. We forfeit our souls every single time we choose to drain ourselves and not replenish ourselves; run on empty rather than stopping and intentionally doing the things that will bring us life; burnout rather than live meaningful, significant, and impactful lives that are enjoyable and life-giving to others. We forfeit the life God intended for us when we lower our souls to functioning as machines rather than living as soulish marvels who require more than a quart of oil or a recharging of our batteries.

We must take custody of our souls. It all begins with making a choice.

■ ■ ■ ■ ■

Questions for Reflection

1. Read Matthew 16:26. Name two or three things you think you've lost along the way as you've lived your life so far.

2. Take a moment to write down words and images to describe the state of your soul right now. Use descriptive words that will help convey how you feel you are really doing. You may find it helpful to use a car dashboard analogy describing different gauges, or possibly seasons of the year—maybe even colors.

3. The writer Annie Dillard states, "How we spend our days is, of course, how we spend our lives." How do you feel about how you are spending your days and your life?

4. *Violence* is a word that you might not have used at first to describe what is going on inside yourself. But what feels violated when it comes to your life—the life you want to live?

5. When you think of taking custody of your soul, what kinds of thoughts do you have?

Notes

1 I've written about my own story and need for transformation in *The Lazarus Life: Spiritual Transformation for Ordinary People* (Colorado Springs, CO: David C. Cook, 2008).

2 Eugene Peterson, "Introduction to Proverbs," in *REMIX: The Message* (Colorado Springs, CO: NavPress, 2003), 870.

3 Walter Trobisch, *Love Yourself* (Downers Grove, IL: InterVarsity Press, 1976), 30.

2

Soul Choices

Turning Your Life Around

We create ourselves by our choices.
—*Søren Kierkegaard*

"Now choose life, so that you
and your children may live."
—*Deuteronomy 30:19*

Moses, the Jewish leader and prophet, was nearing the end of his life. He had delivered his people out of Egypt, led them through the desert, proclaimed the Ten Commandments to them, organized their worship, and brought them to the verge of entering the Promised Land. But would they hold fast to what God had asked of them?

Moses brought the vast crowd of the nation together. He stood before them and reminded the people of the laws of God and of the consequences of their behavior. Then, in a dramatic moment, he declared, "Today I have given you the choice between life and death, between blessings and curses. Now I call on heaven and earth to witness the choice you make. Oh, that you would choose life, so that you and your descendants might live!" (Deut. 30:19 NLT).

In a sense, you and I stand at a similar crossroads. We can keep living in a way that leaves us open to violence against our God-given souls. Or we can choose soul care that will, over time, bring healing, strength, and spiritual well-being. Small choices lead to larger choices. Each day we are faced with choices about how we will live and even a more basic choice: choosing to die before we really live.

Life, death.

Blessings, curses.

The choice is yours.

Eugene Peterson uses a phrase that is revealing when it comes to caring for our souls. Peterson calls it being "able to marshal and direct our energies wisely." It's a paraphrase expression for one of the fruits of the Spirit. We're familiar with it as "self-control" (Gal. 5:23). Caring for your soul is just this: marshalling your energies wisely to live and enjoy life. It's deciding what is important, making space in your life for what really matters.

No one can marshal your energies but yourself. Marshalling your energies wisely involves making healthy choices that foster life within your soul. It is taking the necessary time, investing in lifestyle changes that are life-giving, and living in a way that honors your soul rather than driving it to the precipice like cattle in an old Western movie.

In the chapters to come, we'll be looking at specific choices you can make to care for your soul. Every one of them is crucial. But before that, we need to look at a bigger issue—I call it the choice to choose. You have to decide upon soul care as a priority for your life.

The Power to Choose

Whether we realize it or not, every single day each of us is making choices that impact our lives. Many of these choices may seem small—choices about what we will eat, what work we will do, what relationships we will invest in, and so on. In time, though, we wise up and realize that those "small" choices can impact us for a long, long time. There are no small choices.

Even choosing not to choose to do something is a choice that will inevitably bear fruit. Consider what it can mean to choose not to go to the doctor when you aren't feeling well. Or to choose not to start saving money for retirement.

Each small choice we make in life adds up and creates a wake behind us like that of a boat on a lake. Imagine that my wife asked me to do something for her, such as pay a bill or take out the garbage. If I say, "Honey, I'll deal with it later," my action (or lack of action) will impact both of us. The smell from the remains of last night's dinner might build up in the kitchen. Or we might get a foreclosure notice on our home because I decided to wait to pay the house payment.

The power to be able to choose is a gift that God endowed exclusively to human beings. Flowers, dogs, trees, and fish are not given such a privilege to choose—not like we humans can. A shrimp in the sea, an opossum in the forest, a slug under a rock—they're all alive, yes. Yet not all living things are the same. Our souls, created in the very image of God, distinguish us from other organisms. No other living thing has this sacred distinction.

Choice defines us as soulful beings. It's not just our ability to choose our spouses, our jobs, our houses, our churches, and our favorite flavors of ice cream. It is something more, something we need to explore here because of our need for change.

Choices become a catalyst for us to participate in our own transformation. Remember the words of Paul, author of much of the New Testament, when he said, "Work out your salvation with fear and trembling, for it is God who works in you to will and to act according to his good purpose" (Phil. 2:12–13). Part of our "work" involves making good choices that will breathe life into us rather than choosing to live in ways that deplete us. When we "work out" our own salvation, we are admitting that there are still parts of our lives that need to be saved. Our brokenness through abuse, our shame over our pasts, our guilt over what we did or did not do, our disappointments because of a friend who hurt us—these are the things that we need to still be saved from today.

Becky told me, "I feel like a gas pump that has four hoses running out of my heart. My husband needs one, my two children each get their own, and my work takes the one that is left. But I have no hose running into me to fill me back up."

Tim used a different analogy to make the same point when he told me, "I feel like a coffeepot that everyone pours out to get their own cups filled up. But at the end of the day, the pot has stayed on the burner all day, is empty, and is starting to stink with the smell of burned caffeine."

Do you feel like an empty gas pump or an empty coffeepot? Becky and Tim both made choices to fill their souls back up. You can too. But it's important to know what the choice to choose soul care really means—and what it does not mean.

Self-Help or Soul Care?

I almost feel as though *Soul Custody* should carry a warning label: "Attention: This is not a self-help book."

We love self-help books. Did you know that from one-third to one-half of all Americans will purchase a self-help book in their lifetimes? Included in the self-help section of any major bookstore are volumes on addiction and recovery, diet and fitness, career planning, parenting, personal motivation, self-improvement, psychology, and sexuality and relationships. One New York City, New York, bookstore hosts a quarter of a mile of shelving in its self-help section. *American Bookseller* magazine reported that in one five-year span in the mid 1990s, self-help book sales grew 96 percent.

We love self-help books, and some self-help books are useful. But I repeat: This is *not* a self-help book. This is a book to help your soul find the way to maintain a sense of vitality that will help you thrive, not just survive. You'll find no easy steps here, no surefire formula. Instead you'll find a type of life that God intends for us. It is abundant life within our souls, even though on the outside we may not look like we've reached an ideal state.

The apostle Paul was quite frank about the ongoing trouble in life he encountered. He confessed, "This body of ours had no rest, but we were harassed at every turn—conflicts on the outside, fears within" (2 Cor. 7:5). Paul was describing a situation that many of us can relate to today: a time of soulful challenge, of deep and stressful turmoil. The hymn "Just as I Am" has a verse that speaks to this. Remember singing these old words?

Just as I am, tho' tossed about
With many a conflict, many a doubt,
Fightings and fears within, without …

Charlotte Elliot, the writer of this old hymn, expressed Paul's words honestly and precisely! Yet in the very next sentence, Paul spoke about being comforted by God, about a soulful relationship with a friend named Titus, and about how his joy was rejuvenated.

Caring for our souls is not escaping from trouble. It is not cocooning and burying our heads, ignoring the threats at home or the nuclear age in which we nervously navigate. We might think we could care for our souls better if we lived in a safe place like a convent or monastery. But most of us would only bring our problems there. We blame our lives on the outer world, and we think we are powerless to make choices that will breed life.

Thomas Kelly writes,

We blame it upon the complex environment. Our
complex living we say, is due to the complex world we
live in, with its radios and autos, which give us more
stimulation per square hour than used to be given per
square day to our grandmothers. This explanation by
the outward order leads us to turn wistfully, in some
moments, to thoughts of a quiet South Sea Island
existence, or to the horse and buggy days of our great-
grandparents, who went, jingle bells, jingle bells over
the crisp and ringing snow to spend the day with
their grandparents on the farm. Let me assure you

I have tried the life of the South Seas for a year, the
long, lingering leisure of a tropic world. And I found
that Americans carry into the tropics their same
madcap, feverish life that we know on the mainland.
Complexity of our program cannot be blamed upon
complexity of our environment; much as we should
like to think so....We western peoples are apt to think
our great problems are external, environmental. We
are not skilled in the inner life, where the real roots of
our problem lie.[1]

To face the problems within our souls we must choose to face ourselves. Our inner lives, our souls bear chaos that must be addressed. It is deep within where most of the violence lurks that is killing us and ransacking our souls, who long for peace. Soul custody is caring for, sustaining, fostering, paying attention to the life within us—the only life we have.

Our souls are suffering so much impoverishment because we have wrongly assumed there is an autopilot button we can push to keep going. There's no such button. Our choice is to live or die; to grow or decay; to choose blessing or curse. The soul cannot perform and produce, achieve and acquire without careful choices. It's that simple and it's that profound.

The truth is, our souls require ongoing attention, not a one-time fix-it seminar. To sustain the only life we have, we will need to implement many choices that people have incorporated into their lives for centuries. So what I will offer in this book are not new options or cleverly devised ways to improve your life. The ones you will read of here and consider for yourself are tried, proven, and tested. There is ample witness to the validity of each choice by men and women who wanted the same thing as you and I: life.

The foundation of everything I'm presenting to you is the Bible. It is there we read, "There's nothing like the written Word of God for showing you the way to salvation" (2 Tim. 3:16 MSG). If we are going to talk about saving our lives and not losing them, we need to realize we have great help in the inspired voices of those who lived in trying times of their own and yet found a way to care for the life within them.

This is not self-help. It is God-help. It is a new life.

But we need to choose it before it's too late.

Beyond Living and Dreaming

After all these centuries, after all our attempts to find out how to live, after all the spiritual gurus have voiced their own opinions on how we need to be saved, we need a sure way. Why? Because time is running out for us. Our lives are fleeing even as we sit and read this book.

We could end up on a deathbed of regrets. Perhaps some of us have already made that bed and we're feeling trapped. We must start making the right choices about our life. After all, we get only one life. We will not be given another. This is it—the one, the true, the solitary life you will ever get the chance to live. Much is at stake.

Antonio Machado was a simple schoolteacher who lived out his one and only life in the hills of Spain in the early 1900s. There his passion for life joined an ability to write inspired poetry. In one of his poems he wrote,

Beyond living and dreaming
There is something more important:
Waking up.[2]

Elsewhere, Machado said of Jesus Christ: "All your words were one word: Wakeup!"

Caring for your soul is about waking up to live before you die. It is realizing that eternal life is not just about life in heaven. We live that life beginning right now, right here. The kingdom of God is already at hand and around us, as Jesus reminded us (Luke 17:21). But are we awake to it? To Him? The opposite of being awake to life is being asleep, possibly only slightly aware of what is actually happening to us and in us. It's the living frog put in the boiling pot of water story. Remember? When the frog is first put in the water, he's probably happy. But then the water heats up, and little by little—before the frog knows it—he's dying as the water boils away.

We cannot live our lives on autopilot. We cannot survive with our souls in fifth gear all the time. We will not last. We cannot endure the pace. We cannot sustain our lifestyles because our lives are killing us. We need to live—before we die! Life here and now is a part of God's will for us—not just the one in heaven!

Let me say it again: Our salvation does not just begin in heaven. We are given the choice to be saved right now—to live now, to find new meaning, new purpose, new reason to live—and then to foster, protect, and guard this life. The one and only life for the one and only you.

We get out of life what we put into it.

An Empty Box

Life can be looked at as if it were a box. We want to take something out of the box to make our life work better. For example, if our lives need balance, we will look into the box and try to pull out balance. Or if we want more joy, we reach into the box and look for that. We're bent on finding the secret that will give us what we want.

But life does not work this way. What we want out of the box we must be willing to put into the box. If I want more serenity in my life, then I must do what it takes to put serenity into the box of my life. That might mean, for example, that I must learn to stop hoarding my hateful thoughts toward someone who hurt me. Or if I want more love in my life, I must put love into the box. I must be willing to be a more loving person toward others so that love can come back to me. Or if I want to be a healthy person, I must do something that will move me toward health.

I cannot become what I am not willing to choose right now to begin to become.

Abundant living is a choice that requires a beginning step, a second step, and then many more steps after that. It's time to begin these first steps. Our desires will show us the way.

The Role of Desire

Transformation is not merely rearranging our lives on the surface. If we are concerned about the violence that is happening inside us, if we know we need to stop a particular behavior, if we really want to change our out-of-control lifestyles, we will have to look much deeper, plumb the depths, find the core in which all change takes place.

The place where potential for change resides is inside you. Deep within you is a reservoir of possibility and potential. Go there and you will find longings latent with power and dreams that will motivate you from the inside out. Tap into the realm of your longings, seek to understand your true desires, and discover the place where God meets our needs with His power.

Caring for your soul is about knowing what you really want. Face your own longings and you may see something you did not expect to find. After every diet fails to take off the weight, after all your own efforts break down, after trying to manage your own work schedule and crazy lifestyle, you may find what you really want is something that food or self-effort or a job can't give you. Your desire may be something God put in you to woo you back to a way of living that is far different from how you are living your life right now.

How well do you know the longings of your own heart? What do you really want? The ice cream now or making the choice to live and eat in a way that will honor both body and soul? Desire comes down to where we live each moment of each day. When desire meets the soul, we find the place where motivation is unleashed and action is taken.

But some of us will not hinge our desires to our souls. We will let them lie like sleeping dogs that look comfortable and seem like they don't want to be disturbed. We will not explore our own desires and longings because they are painful to uncover and examine. We will choose to be safe and remain as we are rather than let desires do their deep and disturbing work of unleashing us from lives that we have always known to embrace lives that might be.

As you read on in this book, you'll have to face what you really want in life. You can remain as you are or reach inside for a desire that just might be God-given and meant to make you restless until you walk the path that your longings are calling you to walk.

Here's the deal on desires: The very fact that you want something more in life than what you're experiencing is clear evidence that God is stirring you, helping you want something for yourself. Adele Calhoun writes, "The longing for something more, no matter how weak or crackling with heat, is evidence that God is already at work in your life. You wouldn't want more of God if the Holy Spirit wasn't first seeking you."[3]

It's God's role to woo us, and one of the ways He pursues us is through our desires. Jesus affirmed this when He said, "Blessed are those who hunger and thirst for righteousness, for they will be filled" (Matt. 5:6). To hunger and thirst is to want, desire, crave something to fill us. When we crave what is true for us, we can experience an incomparable filling that is deeply satisfying.

Read the Gospels. You never see Jesus pouring cold water on the desires of the men and women He encountered. He called their desires out, gave them the courage to yearn for what they most wanted. Some wanted freedom. Some wanted wholeness. Some wanted a life richer and better than they had tasted thus far.

Jesus asked blind Bartimaeus a startlingly hope-filled question: "What do you want me to do for you?" (Mark 10:51). It was a God-orchestrated convergence of what Bartimaeus most wanted with what Jesus could do. By unpacking our desires, we will fuel the fire so that our hearts might burn brighter than ever before for God and the life He offers us.

Here's some good news: If you want a different life, it's possible. You don't have to stay the same.

You may be thinking, *I thought I was supposed to slay my desires.* It's true that some of our desires might need to die because not all desires are good. But not all desires are bad, either.

Remember David's exhortation to us? "Delight yourself in the LORD and he will give you the desires of your heart" (Ps. 37:4). The key here is that as we grow closer to God, we actually begin to want what He has wanted for us all along—a life that is deep, full, and satisfying. This is not some justification to ask for material prosperity but instead a call to soulful living that is incomparable to anything we've known. This is profoundly inviting to those who have settled for less than they should, and it is profoundly intriguing to others who need their own desires stirred to want something more in life. The "more" we want is really all that Jesus offers us.

A spirited investigation and soulful inquiry into our longings will show us where the roots of our choices lie. We choose to do or not do something because we *want* to do it. We *desire* to do it. We *long* for it.

Caring for our souls begins by paying attention to what we want in life. Bill will look at his "out of control" lifestyle and have to decide if that kind of ongoing drive is really what he wants after all. Mary will look at her busy life as a mother of five small children and face the pressure of being a homeschool mom and the question of whether she really wants this role. You and I will have to dissect our desires to find out whether we want the ice cream smothered with chocolate sauce and whipped cream and, of course, a bright red cherry or a waistline more in keeping with what our souls are wanting for us.

By facing our desires and longings, we'll find the deeper way to live from our hearts and find the satisfaction promised by the writer of Proverbs: "Souls who follow their hearts thrive" (Prov. 13:19 MSG).

Your Choices

As I clarify the desires that lie within me, as I embrace the privilege
and responsibility of choosing, as I work myself out of a life that
seems to be violent within and around, I can finally grasp the words
that Jesus spoke and start living them.

> *Are you tired? Worn out? Burned out on religion?*
> *Come to me. Get away with me and you'll recover*
> *your life. I'll show you how to take a real rest. Walk*
> *with me and work with me—watch how I do it.*
> *Learn the unforced rhythms of grace. I won't lay*
> *anything heavy or ill-fitting on you. Keep company*
> *with me and you'll learn to live freely and lightly.*
> *(Matt. 11:28–30 MSG)*

It may seem to us that the Christian life described by Jesus, taught
by Paul, and lived out by the early Christian church simply cannot
be lived in our violent culture. Yet here we will find that the life Jesus
wants for us can be lived. We can make the same choices that He and
others have made to foster this life. We can choose to live!

In the chapters that follow, we will look at eight practical choices
we can make to care for our souls and begin to live our lives to the
fullest. These are not the only possible choices involved in soul care,
but they are among the most important for all people. I believe each
one has the power to revolutionize your life.

> *1. Is your life filled with noise, activity, and*
> *confusion? Has it been a long time since*

your spirit was refreshed with stillness and solitude? You need soul solace.

2. *Is your life complicated, distracting? Are your activities, relationships, and possessions keeping you from God? You need* soul focus.

3. *Are you stressed-out, worried, harried? Is everyday life weighing you down and flustering you? You need* soul serenity.

4. *Do your days, weeks, and months seem as endless and futile as a hamster's running on its wheel? Do deadlines and responsibilities always beckon you to do more? Can you not seem to catch a break? You need* soul Sabbath.

5. *Are others trying to make you into the image of the person they want you to be? Do you try to hide or forget the real you—to the point that you aren't even sure who your true self is anymore? You need* soul identity.

6. *Is your work life one of the causes of the soul violence in your life? Is what you are doing for a living far different from the work you have dreamed of to make your life fulfilled? You need* soul vocation.

7. *Can you tell that poor health or a lack of physical fitness is having a negative effect on your soul? Is your attitude toward your body one of neglect or disappointment? You need* soul address.

8. *Are you lonely? Do you wish you had others to accompany you on your journey through life, just as you would like to accompany them? You need* soul companions.

■ ■ ■ ■ ■

Questions for Reflection

1. Read Deuteronomy 30:19–20. As far as your own life is concerned, in what ways do you feel you are making healthy and life-giving choices so far this year?

2. How do you feel about having the power, right, and invitation to make better choices that can breathe life back into you? Do you find that believable? Why or why not?

3. How would you describe the difference between self-help and caring for your soul?

4. When it comes to your life, what do you really want right now? How does what you want impact what you're doing? How about what you might do or not do?

5. Which chapter of this book do you feel yourself already drawn to, and which chapter might you avoid? Why?

Notes

1 Thomas R. Kelly, *A Testament of Devotion* (New York: HarperCollins, 1941), 90–91.
2 Antonio Machado, "Moral Proverbs and Folk Songs," in *In Times Alone: Selected Poems of Antonio Machado*, trans. Robert Bly (Middletown, CT: Wesleyan University Press, 1983).
3 Adele Calhoun, *Spiritual Disciplines Handbook: Practices That Transform Us* (Downers Grove, IL: InverVarsity Press, 2005), 15.

3

Soul Solace

Choosing Stillness

Be still, and know that I am God.
—*Psalm 46:10*

Do everything faster.
—*Tip No. 141 in* 175 Ways to Get
More Done in Less Time *by David*
Cottrell and Mark Layton

Are you a member of a cult? Odds are you probably are. Most of us are. And we're members of the *same* cult, what one author has called the cult of speed.[1]

Today we no longer worry about the survival of the fittest; we are consumed with survival of the fastest. This cult of speed values efficiency over the heart, timely results over truth. It assigns contemplation to the relics of antiquity. What's hot today is fast. Let me do more in less time and I will be content. Until then, I'll work harder.

One professor at a large, prestigious graduate school told me he feels under pressure to have his agenda "filled to the gills every day." When a student asked him for an appointment, he said, "I'm very busy right now. Let me check my calendar to see when I can squeeze you in." He told me saying this to the student made him feel important, and he hoped that the student would see him as such. As the student turned away, the leading professor said, "I felt so ashamed of what I'd just done to him."

The cult of speed—keeping busy and getting it finished faster. This cult's influence is vast, affecting nearly every culture known. Its influence is also deep, invading how we cook (microwave versus slow-cooking gas stoves); how we relax (feeling guilty and honestly not knowing how to relax); and how we work (stress and the threat of job loss making us feel like we have to work more).

The results of living in this cult are devastating to the soul. Why? Because the soul was never designed to operate at the frenetic pace in which we are living our lives. Thus we suffer a kind of sickness of the soul, a malaise deep within us known as "time sickness."[2]

This disease of the soul is threatening because it means we are changing our definition of the "abundant life" promised us by Jesus. To us, having the abundant life means moving faster, getting more done, and producing to survive. Forget about thriving; multitask everything, including your relationship with God. Having a "rich and satisfying life" (John 10:10 NLT) seems like an illusion, not a promise for us now.

Stress is cumulative. Stress builds up rather than dissipates. We forget and ignore this when we live with our time sickness and in the tyranny of the urgent. It builds up and stifles the soul with layer upon layer of residue—and this residue suppresses our spiritual hearts. The lasting effects of living in such a stressed-out state are well documented. Stress has been proven to manifest itself through a wide array of physical problems: heart attacks, gastro-digestive issues, cancer, anxiety disorder, insomnia, and others. These are but a few of the physiological manifestations of living with so much stress. In 2003, stress replaced backache as the number one cause of British workers staying at home due to illness.

Meanwhile, when we feel down, lethargic, or zoned out, we look for the quick fix. We play a song. Take a brisk walk. Take something to numb what this gnawing emptiness inside is trying to alert us to. We try to "recharge the batteries," but the soul is not a battery that can be jump-started.

We need a different approach. We need to make a deliberate choice for the health of our souls. What will it take to breathe life back into our battered souls and connect us again to God?

How to Experience God

The prevailing wisdom, which may not be all that wise, says that being active and committed and attending every seminar we can for our growth, personal development, and spiritual growth is what is good for us. We need to get all we can all the time.

Wrong.

The rhythm of the soul requires us to reexamine how we really learn about God and experience the life He passionately wants for us. We see it expressed in the verse that begins this chapter: "Be still, and know that I am God" (Ps. 46:10). This verse whispers to us the way of the soul—how the soul must live in order to thrive, not just survive.

Thomas Kelly, a Quaker teacher and author, reminds us of the way of the soul in his classic *A Testament of Devotion*, in which he says,

Over the margins of life comes a whisper, a faint call,
a premonition of richer living which we know we are
passing by. Strained by the very mad pace of our daily
outer burdens, we are further strained by an inward
uneasiness, because we have hints that there is a way
of life vastly richer and deeper than all this hurried
existence, a life of unhurried serenity and peace and
power.[3]

We don't have to be Quaker—the people known for their quiet ways and *quaking* in the presence of God—to know we're missing something as we're running faster, harder. What we're missing is life—the life God wants us to live.

Today we might not quake in the presence of God because we won't sit still long enough to give Him a chance. We fidget, squirm, and feel shame because we are not doing more. Our fear is that we might be found out by a human authority who will be disappointed that our schedules are not more crowded with appointments, obligations, and commitments.

Here's the bottom line: A life of prolonged busyness, engaging with people, performing tasks, and expanding your knowledge about God does not help you experience God. More information, no matter how good it is, does not yield a transformed life. Transformation and deep change are ushered in by experiencing God, not just knowing about God. And stillness is required.

Our problem is we don't really know how to be still. We equate it with a night off from the Internet, a "moment of silence" in a jam-packed liturgical service, or time spent in the dark after a storm knocks out our electricity and we have no choice but to talk to each other. Stillness is a practice that the soul needs to experience, and yet, for some of us, learning to be still can be like admitting ourselves into a rehab clinic to detox from the pollutions of the soul that have violated the ways of God.

I believe being still is best defined as slowing myself down—everything from my heart rate to my thoughts. In order to do that I must turn away from the usual. It starts with laptops and iPods and continues to friends, even my spouse. However, my turning away is that I may return to wife and family and work refreshed, renewed.

Stillness is a choice that grants us the gift of coming to our senses—*seeing* through the glass darkly, *listening* for the music of the spheres, *feeling* the presence of God. Without stillness, we have eyes but don't see, ears but don't hear, a pulse but not a life.

At the retreats my wife and I conduct, we see firsthand the absence of stillness in the lives of those who attend. While physically present, the folks are not mentally, spiritually, physically, or emotionally ready to begin a weekend of retreating together. Just because they are there doesn't always mean that they are truly present. Their minds may still be on the unfinished e-mail they left as they jetted out of the office or the meeting that had to be cut short in order to travel to be with us.

Often, while standing in front of a newly arrived group, I will fill a large glass jar with crystal-clear Colorado mountain water and then add to that jar a handful of dirt. I hold the jar up in silence and shake it vigorously for a few seconds. The clear water instantly becomes muddy, brown, opaque. I say, "This is how many of us feel on our beginning time here. Stirred up. Muddy. Confused. Unable to see clearly." Then I put the jar of stirred-up water on a table and say, "As this water sits still without any motion, the dirt will inevitably settle to the bottom of the jar, making the water more clear."

This is what stillness does. Being still helps the soul to feel settled and "centered," to use a Quaker term. Through the stillness, and with time, the soul is better able to see what needs to be addressed, where the real thirst within lies, what the real issues are that need to be explored.

Schola

It's interesting to note that our word *scholastic* is rooted in the Greek word *schola,* which means "free time." The Greeks knew what we must learn. All learning does not happen in rows of school desks or packed church pews. Learning involves ample time that is lingering, unstructured, and unprogrammed—*schola*.

I recently watched my godson trying to catch a grasshopper in the Texas hill country. He stayed entertained for an hour trying to catch the fleeing, flying insect. He squealed in delight when it escaped his grasp. He got on his stomach and tried to get eye-to-eye with the bug. He learned the ways of a bug, and in his *schola*, he learned about the warm grass beneath his belly—perhaps how that grass was different from his carpeted living room back home. The world was his classroom, the bug his teacher.

■ ■ ■ ■ ■

There is far more to your life than the food you put in
your stomach, more to your outer appearance than the

*clothes you hang on your body. Look at the birds, free
and unfettered, not tied down to a job description,
careless in the care of God.*

*And you count far more to him than birds. (Matt.
6:25–26 MSG)*

■ ▪ ■ ▪ ■

Martin Luther, reflecting on the above verses, said, "Let birds become
your teachers and flowers the theologians." Stillness begins with what
Luther and Jesus together said: "Consider."

If considering a flower or bird seems like a waste of time to you,
stop and ask yourself why.

Staring at a blinking cursor on my computer screen is not the
kind of "considering" Jesus had in mind. To consider is to stop, wait,
even linger. It is to pause like Moses did when he first noticed the
burning bush.

By pausing, Moses came to know something. He could have
passed by and said, "That's just the sun's reflection from the desert
rocks." But *schola* dictated the moment, allowing him to consider: "I
will go over and see this strange sight—why the bush does not burn
up" (Ex. 3:3).

What is significant is what the writer of Exodus boldly tells us in
the very next verse: "When the LORD saw that he had gone over to look,
God called to him" (Ex. 3:4). God was waiting for Moses to turn aside,
to pause, to enter *schola*, and to learn something that no tattered page

of the Jewish Holy Scriptures could ever teach him. He experienced God—the God he had learned about. The God of Adam and Abraham conversed with him. Moses' soul would never be the same.

Our souls, too, will be transformed when we learn to practice the old rhythms of the soul.

Stillness + Quiet + Rest + Solitude = Experiencing God

The Gentle Whisper of God

Our world is noisy and so are our hearts. We fear the quiet because it feels "too scary," as one woman recently told me. When I asked her why, she replied, "Because I think thoughts I know I should not think." When I asked her for specific examples, she rattled off without a breath, "Oh, you know, like how much I don't like my life. I hear things like, 'You're miserable. Just end it.' Steve, staying busy means staying alive."

Scott was one of those people I told you about who come to our retreats breathless. His flight was delayed due to thunderstorms, and he felt guilty about arriving late. When I said, "Scott, let's start our time together by enjoying some quiet and silence together," he became agitated and fidgety. When I asked what was wrong, he snapped, "So this is what you're going to make me do—be quiet? I need help. I don't need to just sit here and do nothing!"

Scott arrived in a cultlike trance, bringing his demands to do something, produce, achieve. "I'm done with *quiet,* Steve. It doesn't work for me," he said. He pleaded with me to give him something to do—anything other than to be still.

Maybe like Scott, the prophet Elijah was "done" with quiet. But then,

> *The LORD said, "Go out and stand on the mountain in the presence of the LORD, for the LORD is about to pass by."*
>
> *Then a great and powerful wind tore the mountains apart and shattered the rocks before the LORD, but the LORD was not in the wind. After the wind there was an earthquake, but the LORD was not in the earthquake. After the earthquake came a fire, but the LORD was not in the fire. And after the fire came a gentle whisper. (1 Kings 19:11–12)*

If God were to speak to us as a gale-force wind or an earthquake, we wouldn't need to be quiet. But He usually chooses to whisper. If we want to hear Him, we've got to be quiet.

My retreat guest Scott gave quiet another try, and by the end of the retreat, he had reached a place of spiritual stillness where God could reach him. Quiet is an art that any of us can learn if we try.

The Spiritual Discipline of Rest

Elijah helps us understand stillness in another way.

In 1 Kings 19 we find the prophet at his wits' end. Because he had humiliated the king, a bounty had been put on his head, and he was being pursued. Under threat for his very life, Elijah fled—not as a victor, but as a nomad. Tired. Alone. Exhausted.

Elijah was also so depressed that he "prayed that he might die" (v. 4). What happened next is key to understanding how the soul of a person responds to such stress. We're told that Elijah was ready to throw in the towel. He confessed, "I have had enough."

When the soul is jarred, stirred, and stressed, the way to deal with this is not drugs but stillness and rest. Notice that this is precisely what happened. We're told that Elijah laid down and "fell asleep" (v. 5). After a period of necessary rest, sleep, and quiet, Elijah was provided bread and water that he took and enjoyed. Then Elijah rested again (v. 6). And again he was provided nourishment through simple food and thirst-quenching water.

Rest is grossly underestimated as a spiritual necessity, a tangible and specific way to care for our souls. For Elijah, rest was more than a "power nap." It was at least two days of nothing but sleeping and eating. Sounds like the behavior of royalty or someone who needs to be hospitalized, doesn't it? But why?

After intense periods of output, effort, and expending energy, we are wise to take extended time off to give the soul room to rest, replenish, and renew with good food and good drink. It may seem like this can be done later, when there's time. But the reality for most of us is that there is never time to squeeze in soul care. It must be intentionally scheduled, honored, and prioritized. For Elijah, stillness looked like lots of rest and lots of nourishment before he was ready for the next part of his journey.

I'm not sure many of us would equate rest, sleep, and good nourishment with common spiritual disciplines like prayer and Bible study. But why not? Consider the passionate cry from the heart of Jesus himself in Matthew 11:28–30.

It's difficult for busy people to realize that Jesus was in favor of rest and life that is free and light. What has happened to us—we who have been charmed into the pace of life that leaves us haggard and empty, only able to give of our mutual emptiness to each other?[4]

Tim and Bev came to our retreat just as Jesus described: tired, worn-out, and burned-out on religion. Both were church leaders juggling several roles. They loved God, and their souls were tired out. Sound familiar?

Tim and Bev needed some time to rest, time to rediscover each other, time to explore their regrets of giving their best to the church and having only leftovers for each other. They confessed to me, "The church has hijacked our marriage. We feel forced to give everything to our church life, only to find out we have nothing to give to one another."

In time, Tim and Bev quit blaming the church for choices they had made and practices that had resulted in their marital bankruptcy. They learned, like so many others, that freedom existed to make their own choices about how they would live, serve, work, and enjoy marriage.

You and I must have the courage to give ourselves permission to do what Jesus said we could and should do. So many of us are simply trying to do our best, to do as we are told and led to believe. But until we stop and really examine what Jesus meant here, we will miss caring for our souls. We will run on empty and cruise on autopilot until we crash. No one will give you permission to live like Jesus and do what Jesus did—even embrace the way He lived his life—but yourself.

No human soul is an Energizer Bunny, able to go on and on and on without rest. The soul must stop, learn to be still, and rest.

Alone without Being Lonely

When we're caught up in our cult of speed and afflicted with time sickness, we're engaging with other people and the world endlessly. But a soulful life includes a rhythm of together time and alone time. Even Jesus, after dismissing the needy crowds one day, "went up on a mountainside by himself to pray. When evening came, he was there alone" (Matt. 14:23).

And yet He was not really alone. He was with His Father. Today the Heavenly Father longs to come to meet with each of us as we choose to step away from the world to find Him.

This being alone comes more naturally to some of us than to others.

I am an E (for extrovert) on the Myers-Briggs personality assessment. I love being with people and am energized by them. It's no wonder that as a leader I lead my family, friends, and organizations by having dinners, parties, cookouts, and events. Our home always seems to be the hub of activity.

Recently, though, I have come to believe that my E is really an *unredeemed* E. I say unredeemed because being born with a personality trait that energizes me by people and activities does not mean I need to always be "on"—always available, always surrounded by people.

I've heard some of my fellow extroverts, trying to justify their nonstop lifestyles, say, "That's just the way God made me." Personality may be a reason, but it's not an excuse. Even the most out-there extrovert can come to enjoy periods of solitude and benefit from them.

Regardless of your personality type, let me give you some assurance on an important point: Solitude is not the same thing as loneliness.

People today are plagued with loneliness. We can be lonely in a marriage, lonely at a party, lonely in a megachurch. Loneliness occurs when, no matter how physically near we are to other people, we are left with rumbling feelings that no one really knows us, maybe no one really cares. *They all seem connected, but I'm not. What's wrong with me?* we think.

Solitude is different. It is a deliberate choice we make—like listening to the quiet and getting rested up—that enables us to be still before God. In solitude we distance ourselves from other people temporarily, but we are very much present with ourselves and God. There we can know a closeness with Him that would be impossible to experience in the busyness of our days, which we spend shoulder-to-shoulder with so many people.

Writer Annie Dillard has said that the word *alone* is actually a hybrid made up of two distinct words: *all* and *one*. We can become more "one" with ourselves and God when we learn to embrace the fruit that solitude offers us. The movement to be at one with ourselves and with God, to a place where our hearts are undivided (Ps. 86:11), our mind is at peace (Isa. 26:3), and our souls are content begins with the movement from being lonely to being alone.

Spiritual writers from every generation have agreed on this: Without solitude, we will lose our way. The soul requires the basic nourishment that silence and solitude provide. Without them, we live impoverished. Henri Nouwen tells us,

> *In solitude, I get rid of my scaffolding; no friend to*
> *talk with, no telephone calls to make, no meetings to*
> *attend, no music to entertain, no books to distract,*
> *just me—naked, vulnerable, weak, sinful, deprived,*
> *broken—nothing. It is this nothingness that I have*
> *to face in my solitude, a nothing so dreadful that*
> *everything in me wants to run to my friends, my work,*
> *and my distractions so that I can forget my nothingness*
> *and make myself believe that I am worth something.…*
> *Solitude is not simply a means to an end. Solitude is*
> *its own end. It is the place where Christ remodels us*
> *in his own image and frees us from the victimizing*
> *compulsions of the world. Solitude is the place of our*
> *salvation.*[5]

Take away the "scaffolding" and I am forced to look at my life and see sometimes just how shallow, dependent, and compulsive I can become. Solitude provides for me the great encounter to experience myself and the true God. In that place, there is a knowing that is knowing indeed.

The Honey of Stillness

The call to "be still" is really as dramatic a prophetic cry as that which John the Baptist voiced when he wore the skin of a camel, ate locusts, and drank sweet honey made from desert flowers. The call to choose to be still—the choice to experience the quiet and intentionally leave the crowds of people to taste the honeylike experience of solitude—often falls on deaf ears. But some are learning. I hope I am learning. I hope you are.

Recently I e-mailed a favorite author friend of mine to come to our city to lead a retreat on stillness and being quiet.

He turned me down. His words were "Steve, I'm afraid I can't. I'm trying to live the life I'm talking about." He meant that he had to practice stillness, not just talk about it.

At first I was mad at him. "How can you do that when so many are in need out here?" But as I've sat with his words, I've realized that I need them to find a place in my own soul.

Regrettably, many in the marketplace and ministry have to hit a wall and feel the near loss of their souls before they are jarred into turning things around and learning, perhaps for the first time, to practice the beautiful soul care of stillness.

Taking back our souls from nearly losing them will require the choice of stillness. In stillness and quiet, we gain back what we have lost. Its honey waits in the comb for any of us to taste and enjoy.

■ ■ ■ ■ ■

Questions for Reflection

1. Read Psalm 46:10 carefully. According to this verse, how does a person know God?

2. What's the speed or pace of your life right now? Is it different than the speed you lived at five or ten years ago? Why or why not?

3. What observations can you make about the speed of your workplace, family life, church life, et cetera?

4. How do you normally experience God? If you struggle with the word *experience,* ask yourself why? What other word would you use?

5. What specific challenges arise when you try to be quiet and alone? What happens around you? What happens in you?

Notes

1   Carl Honore, *In Praise of Slowness: Challenging the Cult of Speed* (San Francisco: Harper-SanFranciso, 2004), 3.
2   A term coined by Larry Dossey, an American physician, in 1982.
3   Thomas Kelly, *A Testament of Devotion* (New York: HarperCollins, 1992), 92.
4   Examples of Jesus' own rhythm of work and rest are found in the gospel of Luke, the medical doctor who accompanied Jesus and wrote about his findings. Read Luke 4:42; 5:16; 6:12; 9:18; 11:1; 21:37; and 22:39. It appears that Dr. Luke had a keen interest in healthcare issues, and the lifestyle of Jesus did not escape the doctor's notice.
5   Henri Nouwen, *The Way of Heart* (New York: Ballantine, 1981), 15, 18.

4

Soul Focus

Choosing a Simplicity of Faith and Life

[Don't let your minds] be corrupted
from the simplicity that is in Christ.
—*2 Corinthians 11:3 NKJV*

There is no greatness where
there is not simplicity.
—*Leo Tolstoy*

The Statler Brothers sang, "Things get complicated when you get past eighteen."

Do they ever.

Without our even realizing it's happening, life becomes jumbled—full of things to accomplish, possessions to take care of, obligations to meet. All this can seem like a smoke-filled room, giving us a squeezed-in feeling that smothers the soul.

Consequently, many of us have a yearning for a simpler life. Our yearning, however, is not always realistic.

I was once flipping through a magazine and saw a photo of a cabin in the woods, complete with two rocking chairs on the front porch beside a small table with a potted geranium and a cup of coffee. I instantly wanted to be there. I could almost smell the coffee and hear myself talking with my wife as we rocked side-by-side.

I showed that picture to her and said, "Let's do it. Let's move there and live our lives."

She smiled and said, "Where will the boys sleep when they come home? We need bedrooms for them. And we want grandkids, Steve. Where will the grandkids play?

"You're dreaming," she continued. "Come back to earth. That's an illusion."

I hate it when she's right like that. But her comments did make me wonder if there was wireless Internet access nearby.

Ah, the dream of the simple life! But in this chapter I don't want to talk about illusions but reality, about the kind of simplicity that every follower of Jesus can have if he is willing to do some soul care. We can live in the freedom of a faith uncluttered by religion and a lifestyle uncluttered by greed.

Getting Back Our First Love

Sometimes I feel like someone hijacked the message of Jesus. Everything seems so complicated, so slick, and so much. Is there a way to major on the majors and minor on the minors?

When Jesus described the kind of faith He wants to see in us, He used children as the primary model (Mark 10:13–16). In other words, He wants us to have total loving trust in Him, just like a babe in its mother's arms. Yet many of us have "matured" far beyond that kind of simple trust, and we can hardly imagine allowing children to be our mentors and models.

The truth is, to borrow wording from the apostle Paul, many of us have been "corrupted from the simplicity that is in Christ" (2 Cor. 11:3 NKJV). I confess I'm guilty. But I have found there are some ways we can get that simplicity back. There are ways to have a simple, childlike faith in Jesus even in our complicated world. I'm going to suggest three ways, and the first of them appears in that same verse in 2 Corinthians.

Practicing soul custody in our spiritual life involves not allowing ourselves to be "led astray from [our] sincere and pure devotion to Christ" (NIV). It's obvious Paul knew, as do we, that it's possible to go off course.

This is a recurring theme and warning in the Scriptures. We can start off so well and yet end so tragically. John captures in memorable language the danger of this threat to our souls when he relays the Lord's message to a body of believers in a town called Laodicea.

> *I see what you've done, your hard, hard work, your*
> *refusal to quit. I know you can't stomach evil, that*
> *you weed out apostolic pretenders. I know your*
> *persistence, your courage in my cause, that you never*
> *wear out.*
>
> *But you walked away from your first love—why?*
> *What's going on with you, anyway? Do you have any*
> *idea how far you've fallen? A Lucifer fall!*

Turn back! Recover your dear early love. (Rev. 2:3–5 MSG)

Losing our heartbeat for God is walking away from our first love with Jesus.

I have rarely seen a heart grow cold toward God in a split second. Even those who have experienced the most tragic situations through unjust suffering and heartbreaking crisis rarely walk away from God's embrace swiftly. No, it happens slowly. Over time, the pulse becomes softer and softer and finally almost nonexistent.

Let me ask you a question: If your heart is not beating for God, what is your heart beating for? Whatever it is that makes your heart race and your soul flinch is probably sucking away your first love for Jesus and causing your life to be complicated. Like the tentacles of an octopus, the effects of all of this breathless, complicated living grip and squeeze us. But it is possible to again have love in our hearts for God and the life he wants us to live.

Returning to the simplicity that is in Jesus Christ means having a love that is as passionate today as it was the day we awoke to our need for a Savior to save us from the mess of our lives. That kind of love still warms the heart and makes the soul feel satisfied indeed when we learn to rest in what really matters in this life and let go of the rest.

Can you put your arms about Jesus' neck and just rest there?

Following Jesus

Another way to have the simple faith we yearn for is to focus on Jesus above all—by that I mean Jesus above all other leaders. Jesus' teachings above all competing doctrines. The Jesus life above all other ways of living.

Apart from Jesus, we can't have the life we are searching for. Of course, we may try to gain this life by living our dreams according to the American way … or the English, French, or Brazilian way. Culture has the power to dupe us, to flood us with mixed messages that soak into our souls, making the "good life" seem not only necessary but deserved. But as we see, that life and way is simply not producing for us what we most want and need. We're dying as we try to live this life that seems elusive for us.

The "simplicity that is in Christ" is following Jesus. Jesus said, "I am the way and the truth and the life. No one comes to the Father except through me" (John 14:6). When Jesus offered these words, He offered us more than a direction sign upon life's highway. It was clear that Jesus was offering people the most basic choice they could make in life. By following Jesus as the way, we would know the truth, and these combined would offer us life—the only life worth living. Eugene Peterson reminds us, "The Jesus way wedded to the Jesus truth brings about the Jesus life."[1]

The "simplicity that is in Christ" is found by learning to turn time and time again to the way that Jesus "did" his life and the truth He offered that revolutionized the lives of ordinary men and women who dared listen to Him. And it is accepting the invitation Jesus offered then and continues to offer today to live—to really live with our souls intact, our hearts undivided, and our destination sure.

Following Jesus means following His example, His paradigm for living, His words. Jesus explained it this way in his Sermon on the Mount: "These words I speak to you are not incidental additions to your life, homeowner improvements to your standard of living. They are foundational words, words to build a life on" (Matt. 7:24 MSG).

Today the words of Jesus have too often become add-on words to improve how we are already living. But this was not His intent. He said, "Don't look for shortcuts to God. The market is flooded with surefire, easygoing formulas for a successful life that can be practiced in your spare time. Don't fall for that stuff, even though crowds of people do. The way to life—to God—is vigorous and requires total attention" (Matt. 7:13–14 MSG).

It's true that we are sheep who get lost and who need the nudge and encouragement of the shepherd to get us back on the path we've abandoned for greener grass. But Jesus' invitation, simply put, is this: "Follow me." These two words describe what it means to live out our faith in our everyday lives.

This was the same invitation that Jesus extended to men and women caught in their own webs of trying and trying to make life work but failing to do so. By following Jesus, everything changed for them—and everything changes for us. Giving Jesus total attention and choosing Him means that we now have our bearings. We follow Jesus.

Drawing Near to God

There's yet another way to have simple faith in Jesus. This may be the most basic way of all. It is simply being close to God.

James bids us, "Come near to God and he will come near to you" (4:8). The "coming near" is a movement of our souls to the presence of God. We move and God moves. It's a dance that the soul knows the steps of quite well, a dance described to us for centuries by mystics, poets, and preachers. But here's the deal: What will "coming near" look like for you?

Coming near to God is an act the soul completes to make space for the awareness of God. We do this by practicing much of what I am describing in this book. We create space; open ourselves up, believing that as God spoke to Moses, Ruth, Paul, and Mary, so He will speak to us. Coming near means doing what God said at the transfiguration: "This is my Son, whom I love; with him I am well pleased. Listen to him!" (Matt. 17:5). Coming near means listening. And listening sometimes means keeping your mouth closed so your soul can open up. We choose to be quiet and to be still so that we can know certain things, and one of them is certainly to know that God is moving close to us.

Through coming near to God, we are intimate with Him. The greatest benefit of spiritual intimacy is knowing that we are loved with an everlasting love, that our identity is secure as God's loved sons and daughters, and that we are embarking on a journey involving faith, with a few companions by our sides and heaven as our goal. Nothing less.

To think that our cosmic God would desire proximity with us is one of the fundamental, distinguishing marks of the Christian faith. Buddha's belly is not as inviting as the sheer love and grace of God. Obligatory obedience to Allah is no life-giving duty for the Christian who longs for closeness. And here we get back to the childlike quality of a simple faith.

It was Jesus who offered us the profound title of Father when referring to God. The Aramaic expression a child uses to call his father—*Abba*—is precisely how Jesus and Paul described our approaching God (Mark 14:36; Rom. 8:15). Simple faith says that God more than tolerates us; He desires us. We are lavishly loved by Jesus. We are comforted by His presence through God's Spirit. We do not want (Ps. 23:1–2). In this place all is right with the world and with us.

But it is not only in our faith that we need to come back to "the simplicity that is in Christ." More obviously, and just as importantly, it is in our relationship to wealth and to the things that wealth can buy that we need to find simplicity. As we have seen, following Jesus means leading Jesus' kind of life. And that is most certainly *not* a life burdened by material possessions.

The Deceitfulness of Wealth

In His parable of the sower, found in Mark 4:1–20, Jesus offered an insightful story to help us make sense of the threats to our souls posed by wealth. Here's a story of a farmer who sows his seed on four different kinds of soil. In one part of this story, Jesus explains, "Still others, like seed sown among thorns, hear the word; but the worries of this life, the deceitfulness of wealth and the desires for other things come in and choke the word, making it unfruitful" (Mark 4:18–19).

What started off well ended tragically. The new growth of the seed got choked and became unproductive. Jesus says this happens because of three enemies:

> *1. the worries of life*

> *2. the deceitfulness of wealth*

> *3. the desires for other things*

The combination of those three things is the seedbed of thorny complications that make life so difficult, so complicated, so stressful.

We all know what the lure of greed and materialism looks like. It's everywhere, calling to us all the time.

There are outfitters in Colorado who provide pack llamas for three- to five-day treks through the Rockies. It's a growing business because people these days are less likely to want to carry all their stuff around. So they hire a llama to haul it for them.

Houses in the early part of the twentieth century did not have closets. Rooms had simple wardrobes or shelves and hooks where clothes were placed. Today spacious walk-in closets are among the most requested features of new homes. We need more and more storage space to keep our things. Specialty stores and even careers have come into existence to help people arrange their stuff in color-coded metal, wooden, or plastic assorted-sized bins.

The soul can be deceived, and we have to be alert to this strong possibility. Any soul can be deceived.

It's interesting that Paul said point-blank that a leader of the church should "not [be] a lover of money" (1 Tim. 3:3). A lover of God, yes, but not a lover of money. To love both with so much passion causes a schism in the soul. There simply is not room for both.

Jesus was bold and honest when He ascribed money as a rival god. He didn't even give Satan that status (see Matt. 6:24). But somehow money, possessions, and the significance we give them get all twisted up in our thinking and make the soul feel choked. Slowly our hearts might begin to beat for something else rather than for God, and our first love begins to fade.

Consider Paul's words to young Timothy.

> *Those who crave to be rich fall into temptation*
> *and a snare and into many foolish (useless, godless)*
> *and hurtful desires that plunge men into ruin and*
> *destruction and miserable perishing.*
>
> *For the love of money is a root of all evils; it is*
> *through this craving that some have been led astray*
> *and have wandered from the faith and pierced*
> *themselves through with many acute [mental] pangs.*
> *(1 Tim. 6:9–10 AB)*

Did you catch Paul's warning? "Wandered from the faith …
pierced themselves through with many acute mental pangs." It sounds
like a soul held hostage by a threatening force! The word *acute* means
"sudden, violent, and distressing." Perhaps it's upsetting to realize that
neither Jesus nor any of the writers of the Scriptures gave money a
neutral or benign status. Quite the contrary. And because it is "deceit-
ful," we are lulled into allowing our souls to be choked by its clutch.

Too much of anything can make the soul sick. Simplicity is God's
way of caring for the soul by showing us what is truly needed in the
spiritual life. Without doing the work of living simply, we will only be
weighed down by caring for what we should not care for, stockpiling
what will not last, and living with a divided heart that pulls us apart
rather than giving us freedom to live from the core of our souls.

G. K. Chesterton, an English writer and Christian apologist, said,
"There are two ways to get enough: one is to continue to accumulate

more and more. The other is to desire less." This was precisely Jesus'
point in the parable of the soils and souls: By desiring the wrong
things, we move in a step-by-step dance away from the transforming
love of God.

Jesus put it this way in His Sermon on the Mount.

> *What I'm trying to do here is to get you to relax,*
> *to not be so preoccupied with getting, so you can*
> *respond to God's giving. People who don't know God*
> *and the way he works fuss over these things, but*
> *you know both God and how he works. Steep your*
> *life in God-reality, God-initiative, God-provisions.*
> *Don't worry about missing out. You'll find all your*
> *everyday human concerns will be met. (Matt.*
> *6:31–33 MSG)*

How does Jesus do that? How does he nail us? He obviously
knows that we are going to be "so preoccupied with getting" that we
will go to the edge and put our very souls at risk.

Jesus offers us a prescription for the cure and care of our souls:
Put God first. By putting God first in our lives, we get our souls back.
We choose to care for what God cares for. We live for what God
lives for. And by doing so, the simple truth becomes our everyday
reality—our "everyday human concerns will be met." It's that simple.
It's that true. It's that life-giving.

Maintaining simplicity is about learning how to move from
worry to trust, from anxiety to faith, and from apprehension to
peace. When we move toward simplicity, we are literally moving

our minds' attention to focus on what really matters. As T. S. Eliot prayed, "Lord, teach us to care and not to care."

Letting Go

Adele Calhoun describes simplicity as taking action so that "I uncomplicate and untangle my life so I can focus on what really matters." When life and the soul become so cluttered with stuff, options, schedules, and demands, the cry of the soul is "less!" In simplicity we "cultivate the great art of letting go. Simplicity aims at loosening inordinate attachment to owning and having. Simplicity brings freedom and with it generosity."[2]

The nature of our unredeemed souls is to grab and hold on to what we want. As we grow in our lives, we grow in our understanding that we can relax our fingers from clutching everything and everyone so tightly. Simplicity's greatest invitation is for us to practice trusting in the sovereignty of God. We trust by letting go. We express our faith in using only the necessities in life. It is living our lives by the basic few ingredients that are necessary to truly live. In doing this, less becomes more. The posture of the simple life stands in the face of the lie, illusion, and myth that more, not less, is more.

It is not easy to keep a simple soul. It takes far greater faith to believe that less is more than to believe that more is more. Simplicity is a paradox of sorts because to maintain a simple soul and life, one must work at it. Why? Because from the beginning we grab what is not ours, hoard more than we can safely keep, clutch what seems fleeting, and stash what we are convinced we might need someday. Cluttered lives make the spiritual journey cumbersome.

When I travel I often do so with only a backpack. I can move quickly through airports and never have to check my luggage. I place my clothes, shoes, toiletries, and books into my pack, and off I go on some weekend event or speaking engagement. I've noticed, however, that the longer I am away from home, the heavier my pack gets. I buy another book at the airport. I pick up a magazine and add a water bottle and maybe a snack. While I'm at my destination, I might find something my wife would enjoy, so I get that and put that in. Though I started out intending to travel lightly, I have a hard time maintaining that simplicity. I have to keep working at it.

Spiritual writers talk about detachment as an exercise to keep the soul strong and the desire for things in check. Detachment is freeing your soul by letting go of the power that people, things, and sometimes places have on you. It's the exercise of beheading the dragons that cause you to clutch a thing too tightly, hold on to a person too closely, or grip money or possessions too firmly. Detachment is the process of letting go.

All of life can be seen as a continual exercise in letting go of successes to find greater significance in life and letting go of relationships that are not healthy. Throughout life we let go of so much, including our children, who eventually grow up, spread their wings, and leave the nest. As we age we let go of some of the most basic forms of control that we think make us human. In the end we even let go of our bodies.

Learning through detachment can be a healthy, life-giving, soul-sustaining realization that leads to many "aha!" moments. We realize, "I really don't need this. I can thrive without it." Here we learn to give ourselves the space we need to be ourselves, the space we need to go back to the basics. We learn to unclutter our souls every time we are courageously willing to look underneath and see those dark places where the roots grow that cause us to grip, hoard, hold onto, and refuse to let go. Writer Wendell Berry reminds us of Henry David Thoreau's wisdom: "As Thoreau so well knew, and so painstakingly tried to show us, what a man needs most is not a knowledge of how to get more, but a knowledge of the most he can do without, and of how to get along without it."

As stated by the protagonist in Flannery O'Connor's short story "A Good Man Is Hard to Find," Jesus throws everything off balance. One of the things it seems we all try to balance and justify is our need of things. As Jesus shows up more and more in our lives, though, we will grow to feel more off balance and forced to rethink everything. This is good for the soul, though, and does not have to be thought of as threatening. He does not do this to us with a whip; He does it with grace, always with grace.

Living more simply does not begin by going through our closets and having a yard sale or listing on eBay what we've decided we don't need anymore. Living simply begins with a choice to look inside—at the soul. The inward look helps us explore holdouts—places and attitudes within us that still need to hear about bondage and attachment to things that grip us, stuff that accessorizes the external but leaves the internal spaces of our souls barren and empty. If we do not allow the choices that simplicity confronts us with, we become even more out of control. It becomes what noted author Richard Foster has called "psychotic." Everything becomes turned around so that "covetousness we call ambition. Hoarding we call prudence. Greed we call industry."[3]

Viewing life and faith in such a way makes for a toxicity that infects the heart, goes systemic, spreads like wildfire, and becomes the culture that we accept, live in, tolerate, and applaud. Simplicity is the solution. As Chesterton said, we begin to "desire less." That is, we desire less stuff, but more of Jesus!

Free at Last

Have we forgotten the benefits of embracing simplicity of life and faith? One of the main benefits of embracing a simple life is the freedom we find by untethering ourselves from stuff. The old Shaker song says it best:

> *'Tis the gift to be simple, 'tis the gift to be free,*
> *'Tis the gift to come down where we ought to be,*
> *And when we find ourselves in the place just right,*
> *'Twill be in the valley of love and delight.*
> *When true simplicity is gain'd,*
> *To bow and to bend we shan't be asham'd,*
> *To turn, turn will be our delight,*
> *Till by turning, turning we come round right.*[4]

Unadorned by complex living, the Shakers have much to teach us today. Freedom comes as we embrace the gift to be simple. We are able to "come down where we ought to be" and live more humbly. It's interesting that the word *humble* is rooted in the word *humus*, which refers to the rich, dark, earthy material that is brimming with life-giving substance to living things that are planted in its rich soil,

Finding oneself in a "place just right" is the journey we are in search of—one that leads us through the clandestine and labyrinthine ways of recognition, security, power, "making it," and a false life capturing of our souls. The song speaks of "turn, turn will be our delight," evoking images of clay on the potter's wheel that is being worked out, reformed, and reclaimed as a loving potter turns the wheel to have just enough speed and friction to cause the internal change that is needed. This is the work of living with simplicity in mind and heart. It's a part of the paradox of which I spoke earlier.

Achieving simplicity is not always easy, especially in our wealthy and materialistic culture. It's a work we do with God as He turns us on His wheel. But as unnecessary religious add-ons and burdensome possessions are removed from us, what's left is a soul that finds itself in that "place just right."

■ ■ ■ ■ ■

Questions for Reflection

1. Read 2 Corinthians 11:3. Describe "the simplicity that is in Christ" in your own words. How have you experienced your own mind being "corrupted" from this simplicity?

2. The author describes three enemies that can choke the soul and make life unproductive. Which enemy most threatens your soul and why?

3. In what ways do you experience yourself being preoccupied with getting more or getting ahead? What would it look like for you to "not be so preoccupied with getting"?

4. Most of us desire a life that's less complicated and untangled from the cares of life. Explore specific ways to lessen the complications in your life by 10, 20, or even 50 percent. What would you need to do or stop doing?

5. The author states, "It takes far greater faith to believe that less is more than to believe more is more." What's your reaction to this statement? Do you believe it? If not, why not?

Notes

1 Eugene Peterson, *The Jesus Way: Conversations on the Way Jesus Is the Way* (Grand Rapids, MI; Wm. B. Eerdmans Publishing Company, 2007), 4.
2 Adele Calhoun, *Spiritual Disciplines Handbook* (Downers Grove, IL: InterVarsity Press, 2005), 74.
3 Richard Foster, *The Celebration of Discipline* (New York: HarperCollins, 1998), 81.
4 Composed by Elder Joseph Brackett in 1848. Bracket was a Shaker who lived in Maine as a farmer and songwriter.

5

Soul Serenity

Choosing to Detox from Stress

Half our life is spent trying to find
something to do with the time we have
rushed through life trying to save.
—*Will Rogers,* Autobiography, *1949*

When anxiety was great within me, your
consolation brought joy to my soul.
—*Psalm 94:19*

The UN (United Nations) *Stress Management Booklet*, a manual used
to train peacekeeping workers throughout the world, defines stress
as "the physical and psychological process of reacting to and coping
with events or situations that place extraordinary pressure upon a
human being."[1] The UN offers extensive training for peacekeeping
forces to learn how to cope with stress in war zones, hostile situations, and humanitarian crises. Most of us, however, never get this
kind of training despite the fact that we face, live with, and endure
our own seasons of stress.

At a restaurant last week I overheard a girl who could not have been older than eight say to her mom, "I am so stressed-out. You've got to do something."

The mother, trying to be attentive to the daughter's public melt-down, said, "Honey, big girls don't cry. Suck it up and order your lunch."

Whether we are five or fifty, many of us learn to suck up or stuff down our stress. And where does it go? Unresolved stress gets deposited right into our souls—the deepest part of ourselves.

The Bible refers to stress and distress more than one hundred times. For example, the apostle Paul said, "This body of ours had no rest, but we were harassed at every turn—conflicts on the outside, fears within" (2 Cor. 7:5). Maybe this was what the little girl was feeling at the restaurant. Maybe this is what we are feeling.

The busy executive, the mid-level manager, the high school teacher, the stay-at-home mom—we all face our own stress-makers each and every day. The demands of our roles in life affect the soul. Like a sponge we soak up what we experience around us and look for ways of letting it all out. When we are squeezed too tightly or jarred, we leak at best and spew at worst on those around us—all the stuff that has built up inside our impressionable souls. Stress consumes physical, emotional, and mental energy.

Ted explained it to me this way: "I feel like everyone is sucking the life out of me. It's nearly killing me."

Maybe it really is! That was Ted's cry for help to de-stress his life.

What most of us forget is that stress is both residual and cumulative. Layers and layers of prolonged stress affect every aspect of our lives, and if not dealt with, lead to burnout—where coping skills and fundamental ways of dealing with stress are short-circuited in a person's soul. There is no margin, no reserve, nothing to pull from with which to deal with what is happening around and in you.

John confessed to working sixty-hour weeks for years. He said he was "moving up" in the company, but he confessed to me that he was losing his interest for anything but work. It consumed him. E-mail became a constant way to keep a deal moving long after he had left the office and gone home to his wife and three preschool children. He dropped out of his church's small group because, as he said, "This is my time to really make it."

The problem is John may not "make it" at all. He's coming undone. He's angry and resentful. He wakes up at four a.m. and can't get back to sleep, so he gets an early start on his work. He's dealing, not merely with stress, but with cumulative stress. And it's eating him up.

This kind of ongoing stress leads to lingering effects on the soul. Physical exhaustion, inability to sleep, nightmares, depression, change in eating habits, irritability, anger explosions, withdrawing from meaningful relationships, shrinking back from engaging in meaningful conversation, a feeling of emptiness, sexual dysfunction, and escapist thinking all manifest in the soul. When not properly dealt with, stress manifests itself in dangerous ways: high blood pressure, panic and anxiety disorders, heart disease, gastric disease, and even some forms of cancer. In extremely stressful situations, faith sometimes becomes mute, prayers nonexistent. Spiritual dryness often results from long seasons of exposure to various forms of stress. The ripple effect of this is enough to disturb every person around the stressed-out person. A team of colleagues or a family can become paralyzed, lost in knowing what to do when someone is gripped by stress.

And you? What are you feeling during these days of economic challenge, social change, and international war? Are you seeing your dreams erode like sand at the beach? Are you suffering the silent stress of being overworked and underpaid? Do you have pain in your lower back, tension with your child, conflict with your spouse, and pressure at your job?

There is hope to be found in these areas of your life. You can reduce the stress in your life and cultivate the fruit of serenity—to the everlasting benefit of your soul. But there are wrong and right ways of going about dealing with your stress.

Soul Care for the Stressed-Out

Pete sought help for his stress by getting massages to relieve his tension. But he was not prepared for what happened. He explained to me, "It developed into an addiction for me to the point that I *had* to have one. And then one thing led to the next, and sex got to be a part of it. But the sex meant nothing."

His wife didn't agree when she found out about Pete's attempts to find relief.

When stress is not dealt with properly, we can do bizarre, crazy, and never-before-considered things to relieve the pressures we feel. When the dam of unresolved stress bursts, we tend to act out, sometimes doing the unimaginable.

That's why the most important thing to remember is where we take our stress: to God. He'll understand it and know what to do about it.

The Psalms are filled with pleas and prayers for relief from stressful situations. One of David's prayers speaks of the effects of living with so much unresolved stress.

> *Be merciful to me, O LORD, for I am in distress;*
>   *my eyes grow weak with sorrow,*
>   *my soul and my body with grief.*
> *My life is consumed by anguish*
>   *and my years by groaning;*
>   *my strength fails because of my affliction,*
>   *and my bones grow weak. (Ps. 31:9–10)*

David described what unresolved stress does to us. It weakens us, fills us with sorrow, has a physical impact on us, sets off unspeakable inner turmoil, and zaps energy and vitality.

But David did the right thing. He took his concern to God.

Sadly though—and this grieves me—it doesn't necessarily mean we can find the answers in some of our Christian communities. In my experience the answers about stress we sometimes hear in the Christian community are shallow and hurtful, only compounding the burden. I'll share two examples.

Karen, a schoolteacher with a demanding class, went to see her pastor for what she hoped would be wise counsel to deal with her stress. She was simply told to read her Bible more and pray more often. Karen felt nothing but shame when she heard this because the Bible's pages seemed blank, and her prayers felt unanswered.

I believe Karen primarily needed someone to listen. Fortunately, she began meeting with a group of other women in her church, a group in which Karen felt listened to and cared for. After a season with the group, Karen was gradually able to read her Bible and feel as if there was really something in it for her. She even wanted to pray again.

At the height of the Iraq War, our oldest son served in the heat of the conflict. His job at that time was to keep the Coalition forces stocked and well supplied. That meant he coordinated convoys that delivered arms, water, and food to base camps.

Thousands of miles away, I would awake to the news of more bombings, convoy attacks, and death as I watched the television, powerless to do anything but worry. The stress of being a father with a son at war was my toughest assignment yet. Prayer helped some. But I could not process my feelings much because no one in my circles had their own flesh and blood in the war. I felt isolated. I could not sleep at night and couldn't stop worrying during the day.

The ongoing anxiety I lived with was not helped by some well-meaning friends who sent me notes and e-mails that said things like, "Christians should not worry," and "It is sinful to be so concerned." And then there was this unforgettable voicemail: "How can you, as a Christian leader, become so consumed by fear? Don't you believe in the sovereignty of God?" To add to my own stress came the shame of not being able to handle it well. Many nights I thought, *I'll eat some Double Stuf Oreos. That will help.*

It didn't though.

Then one friend I had not seen in years wrote an e-mail sharing his similar feelings of concern and anxiety when his daughter served as an army nurse treating wounded soldiers in a war zone. He closed his note with this: "Steve, I simply offer you the psalmist's words when he, too, was gripped by fear and anxiety. He said, 'When my heart became anxious, your consolation brought joy to my soul' (Ps. 94:19). Love, Roger." In that single verse I found room in my heart for both my anxiety and God's peace. I began to feel some comfort rather than feeling so stressed-out.

It seems our tendency might be to try to fix our stressed-out friends by quoting a verse, offering a book to read, or suggesting a message to listen to on the Internet. What seems to help more is to simply listen to our friends and let them just talk, simply getting out what is stressing them on the inside. Consolation comes from being listened to, not in watching a friend try to fix what sometimes cannot be fixed.

Gotta Have Rhythm

Some people, in trying to help others with stress, urge them to seek balance in their lives. But I have come to the conclusion that balance is not really what we need. The word *balance* conjures up the mental image of the circus act in which a man places china plates on waving rods. His act is to keep all the plates spinning so that none of them might come crashing down. I've watched that act, and lived that life, and it all felt like a circus life to me.

There is a better way for the soul. It's called *rhythm*. Living with a sustainable rhythm is one of the most important aspects to coping with stress and caring for our souls.

We experience that out-of-control feeling about life when everything around us begins to move too fast. We can't stop because we can't find the breaks. Maybe there are no breaks. We give out, burn out, and start standing out as someone who can't cope. Multitasking seems futile. Going to bed sounds better.

God created the world with a rhythm by which we work for six days followed by a day of rest. We will consider that rhythm at length in the Sabbath chapter. But it's also true that human beings need a rhythm of rest every single day. We need to take breaks, enjoy meals, and get sleep at night so that our bodies may be replenished. We know that the body and the soul cannot thrive when the soul is empty. Rhythm allows each person to engage, then disengage; be involved, then withdraw; work and contribute, then rest and recover.

Nature rests under winter's blanket of snow and cold. Fields rest when the growing season is over. Bears hibernate; snakes shed their skins; animals mate according to a natural rhythm. But the human soul sometimes defies the rhythm that God intended. "We mock the seasons by eating imported strawberries in the middle of winter and hot cross buns, once an Easter treat, all year round. With cell phones, Blackberries, pagers and the Internet, everyone and everything is now permanently available," says Carl Honoré in his remarkable book *In Praise of Slowness: Challenging the Cult of Speed*.[2]

To recognize and live according to God's rhythms fosters and nourishes life. To ignore and defy this soulful imprint of ebb and flow says in the end, "I know best. I know what I need to do and want to do." Everything gets twisted when rhythm is ignored. The soul gets kinks that cannot be easily untwisted through years and years of doing life our own way.

The world's wisest man during his generation, Solomon, shared some wise words about rhythm.

> *There's an opportune time to do things, a right time*
> *for everything on the earth:*

A right time for birth and another for death,
A right time to plant and another to reap,
A right time to kill and another to heal,
A right time to destroy and another to construct,
A right time to cry and another to laugh,
A right time to lament and another to cheer,
A right time to make love and another to abstain,
A right time to embrace and another to part,
A right time to search and another to count your
losses,
A right time to hold on and another to let go,
A right time to rip out and another to mend,
A right time to shut up and another to speak up,
A right time to love and another to hate,
A right time to wage war and another to make peace.
(Eccl. 3:18 MSG)

What rhythm allows us to ask ourselves is this: What time is it for my soul right now? What does my soul need at this particular time? Living with this question and having the courage to ask it repeatedly of ourselves and those we love helps create a redeemed culture that chooses life over drivenness, recovery over burnout, and serenity over perpetual anxiety.

Developing and living with a sustainable rhythm is our souls' real work. This often begins with honest, ongoing conversations, revisiting this topic regularly. Every Sabbath you can ask yourself and your family, "Has the pace in which I have lived this week been good for me? Us? You? How can next week, month, or year be different and more life-giving?" These conversations become ways to share your heart and soul stirrings over what is good and what is not.

Of course there are seasons of sheer engagement in our work because of deadlines and situations that might be out of our control. But even surrendering control of the speed of your life might be more in your grasp than you ever realized.

The Secret to the Christian Life

Adele Calhoun, an author and spiritual director, reminds us that living with rhythm influences the speed in which we live our lives right now.

> *We can get so busy doing urgent things and so preoccupied with what comes next that we don't experience now. Afraid of being late, we rush from the past to the future. The present moment becomes a crack between what we did and what we have yet to do. It is virtually lost to us. We don't get to our futures any faster if we hurry. And we certainly don't become better people in haste. More likely than not, the faster we go the less we become.[3]*

Hurry becomes a stress bomb that can explode at any time, injuring our souls and causing collateral damage to those closest to us. When we value efficiency over health, expediency over doing things well, and speed over soul, we have committed a great sin against ourselves and against the God who created and sustains life. Speed is spiritually deadly to the follower of Christ.

Dallas Willard was asked, "What is the secret to the Christian life?"

He responded, "Ruthlessly eradicate hurry from your life."

This is a prophetic call to stand up against culture's values and seek to live in a way that honors God and the soul. The apostle Paul offers us this challenge when he says,

> *Here's what I want you to do, God helping you:*
> *Take your everyday, ordinary life—your sleeping,*
> *eating, going-to-work, and walking-around life—*
> *and place it before God as an offering. Embracing*
> *what God does for you is the best thing you can*
> *do for him. Don't become so well-adjusted to your*
> *culture that you fit into it without even thinking.*
> *Instead, fix your attention on God. You'll be*
> *changed from the inside out. Readily recognize*
> *what he wants from you, and quickly respond to*
> *it. Unlike the culture around you, always dragging*
> *you down to its level of immaturity, God brings the*
> *best out of you, develops well-formed maturity in*
> *you. (Rom. 12:1–2 MSG)*

This message about the rhythm of life and dealing with the speed at which we are going is one that is applicable to every one of God's children. It's applicable on my street in Colorado Springs, Colorado, or around the world in Calcutta, India.

Time in the Motherhouse

Mother Teresa's work among the poor in southern India is well-known. In a fascinating book about her life and work titled *Mother Teresa: Come Be My Light*, we learn only through a footnote how Mother Teresa developed a regular rhythm that she implemented not only for herself but also for the order she established. Here we learn a powerful way to cope with ongoing stress in the marketplace and ministry.

Before you react too strongly to Mother Teresa's rhythm and say, "This is simply not possible for me," consider the dire situations of her ongoing work with the dying, socially rejected, and marginalized men and women, and the abandonment that these people lived in and the sisters worked in. Mother Teresa said,

> *The Sisters shall spend one day in every week, one week in every month, one month in every year, one year in every six years in the motherhouse, wherein contemplation, and penance together with solitude she can gather in the spiritual strength, which she might have used up in the service of the poor. When these Sisters are at home, the others will take their place in the Mission field.*[4]

Mother Teresa established a regular rhythm for ongoing, hard, and demanding work. Sisters would work for six days in the gutters and despicable places in Calcutta, then leave for one day away in the "Motherhouse," a retreat that was beautiful, restful, clean, and away from the poverty. There the Sisters enjoyed time together, laughing, singing, and enjoying a good meal. They also experienced the blessings of solitude. As you can see, the rhythm she prescribed involved one week a month away, one month a year away, and one year every six years away. This rhythm established a life-giving, soul-honoring method for people to give, serve, and help—but also one through which they themselves were given to, served, and helped!

Stress Treatments

You may not belong to a religious order or have a "Motherhouse" to go to. But the good news is that most stress can be managed. By implementing some guidelines—such as getting enough sleep and rest, eating healthy, exercising regularly, developing satisfying friendships, and laughing at ourselves—we can learn to manage and cope with stressful situations in our lives.

Various factors make stress a very individual and somewhat unpredictable phenomenon; it's impossible to formulate a one-size-fits-all way of dealing with stress. Remember, each soul is unique and fearfully made, and we should resist efforts that offer cookie-cutter remedies to help people cope. Some of our uniqueness includes our education, past experiences in life, learned skills, age, degrees of physical fitness, and our own understanding of self-love, self-respect, and soul care.

What is important is to begin recognizing your own soul's way of dealing with stress, then learning to face it. In learning to cope and de-stress your own life, you are caring for your soul and honoring the way God made you.

The American Red Cross also trains workers in coping with the stress that workers face in natural disasters, terrorism, and other crises. Their advice for learning how to cope with stress is practical.

1. *Use your personal resources fully: social network, sufficient leisure activity.*

2. *Know yourself: your resources, your limits, your stress reactions.*

3. *Share – communicate – be clear: Find someone to share your doubts, fears, and disappointments with; express your needs; say "no"—to unreasonable work demands, etc.*

4. *Support each other: Show that you care for your colleagues and listen to them. Avoid criticizing or playing down their remarks. Be alert to changes in behavior and propose activity if necessary (e.g., take a long weekend off).[5]*

Surely we as believers can at least do what the Red Cross does. What if pastors and leaders in the church knew the hearts of their people as well as they knew the cutting-edge message of the month? What if church became *the* place for people to share and listen and bear one another's burdens and stresses? What if our churches were as intent on being a refuge as they are being relevant?

When we listen to one another, we offer a safe place where the one who speaks will be accepted—not judged, but loved. Not rejected or tolerated, but welcomed. When we find these kinds of ears to listen to us, we will find stress melting and flowing out of us. The simple act of listening to a person talk it out is sometimes that greatest yet simplest way of loving someone well and deeply. When we listen well, we give our hearts to receive, our minds to process, and our souls to share the journey with a friend in need. This is really the action of being hospitable to a person who needs simply to be heard. In that act of being hospitable, we are in fact offering ourselves and the space we share to become a hospital—a place of healing and acceptance.

The words *cure* and *care* are related. To be cured meant that you would be cared for, that you would get the attention you needed to become healthy once again. To extend the care of the soul to weary friends who are stressed-out and burned-out means that we offer them a place to be both cured and cared for—simply by being present, paying attention, and listening to their story.

This gives new and needed meaning to Jesus' own words about how we should treat one another when He said the following in his parable of the sheep and the goats.

> *Then those "sheep" are going to say, "Master, what are*
> *you talking about? When did we ever see you hungry*
> *and feed you, thirsty and give you a drink? And when*
> *did we ever see you sick or in prison and come to you?"*
> *Then the King will say, "I'm telling the solemn truth:*
> *Whenever you did one of these things to someone*
> *overlooked or ignored, that was me—you did it to me."*
> *(Matt. 25:37–40 MSG)*

Today the "overlooked and ignored" might well be the stressed-out man or woman who sits in front of you at worship and who is there physically but whose soul is vacant because of stress, stress, and more stress. It might be the child whose father works seventy hours a week and church is the only time they actually sit together in the entire week. It might be the woman who carries her three preschool children into the church nursery alone because her husband is out of town and she is simply trying to do all the right things, and it is too much, too hard, and too draining.

Stress need not have its way with our souls. Let us help one another, and let us help ourselves, to find the serenity that God desires for us.

"Now may the Lord of peace himself give you peace at all times and in every way" (2 Thess. 3:16).

Ten Stress Busters for Your Soul

1. *Practice the spiritual discipline of slowing down. Begin a meeting with a few moments of silence; practice silence before you have a family meal to allow each person a few moments to collect their thoughts; share or journal about how you might eradicate hurry from your life in the next day, week, or month.*

2. *Seek to explore what is contributing to your stress. Identify the sources of stress and seek to make a 20 percent improvement in de-stressing your life in specific ways. For*

example, if the drive to work is stressful, explore how you can leave earlier or later to avoid the traffic. Seek to make small choices that will lead to bigger steps in living without so much stress.

3. *Park in the parking place that is the farthest from your destination, not closest. Pray as you walk. Talk it out with God.*

4. *How can you incorporate more humor in your life? It's a proven fact that laughing is a stress buster. Watch a hilarious movie once a week. One missionary I know bought DVDs of an old television series. He watches it once a week with his family and friends and says, "It's the day I look forward to the most when I can relax and laugh with my family and friends!"*

5. *Decide to join what is called the slow food movement. Decide not to eat fast food for a month. Instead, enjoy meal preparation as a soulful, life-giving, and even spiritual exercise. Monitor the difference, if any.*

6. *Go to bed thirty minutes earlier every night for a month and evaluate how you feel.*

7. *Do something that gives you life every day. Work with the question, "What makes me come alive?" and practice it.*

8. *Choose one day a week, perhaps your Sabbath, not to check voice mail, e-mail, or use any form of technology. Give all electronic things a rest.*

9. *Become less available to people's demands and more available to the choices that lead to caring for your soul. What choices thus far in this book seem doable for you? What would you specifically like to work on and implement in your life in the next thirty days?*

10. *Walk thirty minutes five days a week at a steady pace and monitor how you feel after thirty days of practicing this.*

■ ■ ■ ■ ■

Questions for Reflection

1. Read 2 Corinthians 1:1–11. What's one example of comfort and trouble coexisting in your life? Paul recounts a very stressful situation in verses 8–11. Describe the "great pressure" Paul experienced

and how this made him feel. How did God deliver
Paul from this situation?

2. How have you experienced the residue and
   cumulative effects of stress in your life over the
   past twelve months?

3. What do you consider to be the three greatest
   sources of stress in your life right now? Explain.

4. How does the speed of your life affect the state of
   your soul? What role does hurry have in your life
   and lifestyle?

5. Describe a rhythm of living that you would like to
   experiment with for the next twelve months. What
   do you want to do daily, weekly, monthly, quarterly
   and annually to care for your soul? Who is an
   encourager you can share this with—someone to
   help you and pray for you during this time?

Notes

1 *UN Stress Management Booklet,* (New York: The United Nations Department of Peace-keeping Operations, 1995), 26.
2 Carl Honré, *In Praise of Slowness: Challenging the Cult of Speed* (New York: HarperCollins, 2004), 35
3 Adele Calhoun, *Spiritual Disciplines Handbook* (Downers Grove, IL: InterVarsity Press, 2005), 79.
4 Mother Teresa, *Come Be My Light* (New York: Doubleday, 2007), 345.
5 *Managing Stress in the Field* (Geneva, Switzerland: International Federation of Red Cross and Red Crescent Societies, 2009), 9.

6

Soul Sabbath

Choosing to Cease the Insanity

If you call the Sabbath a delight and the
LORD's holy day honorable, and if you honor
it by not going your own way and not doing
as you please or speaking idle words,
then you will find your joy in the LORD.
—*Isaiah 58:13–14*

"How did we get so terribly lost in
a world saturated with striving and
grasping, yet somehow bereft of joy
and delight? I suggest that it is this:
We have forgotten the Sabbath."
—*Wayne Mueller*

Have you noticed there is little, if any, ceasing in our 24/7 world?

Technology has made it possible to always be available to more information, breaking news, and greater possibilities. We are always on, always wired, always mindful that the next phone call, e-mail, or tweet might hold *the* opportunity that could change our lives.

Being so available sets us up to live our lives in the illusion that we are more important than we actually are. We think, *I might be needed. I need to be available. I may know something that someone else wants.*

Well, maybe so. But there's something else we need to know about our unceasing spiritual, emotional, and physical availability: It is killing us.

Consistent availability to people and the world is one of the greatest threats to our soul. When we are always on alert, our souls never get the opportunity to settle. There is an extra beat within the four red chambers of our hearts that keeps our adrenaline levels up. We might miss out on something. Someone might get ahead of us. They might get the deal and we will lose. The early bird still gets the worm, right?

John and Karen, a couple I counseled, are in need of soul care in this area.

John's a financial planner. Due to the havoc in the economy, he is always searching for information, tips, and clues to help his clients avoid financial catastrophe. The problem, however, is that the stress John is navigating through and absorbing into his own soul is wreaking emotional chaos at home.

Karen described it to me this way: "We lie in bed together, but the glow of the computer screen reflecting in John's face is not what I want to see before drifting off to sleep. He lies there, computer on his stomach, clicking this, Googling that, and this cyber mistress is ruining our lives." Karen was describing his obsession with the news—an obsession he's developed so he can be on top of his game for his clients at breakfast meetings.

Karen went on: "He works all day in a heightened state of alertness of deals and loss and comes home for a quick meal, tucks the children in bed, and he's at work again by nine p.m. He's a stranger to me."

John realizes the problem as well. He feels degraded to being a slave to work. With no ceasing, John is losing his soul. He told me, "I'm out of control, and there's no way out."

We were not created to always be *on*, to always be available. We were not fashioned to always be aware of everything around us all the time. Constant availability is going to do us in. Even God rested one whole day. Why do we find it so hard to do the same? We are killing our hearts by chasing time as our new rival god—now more precious than gold, more valuable than silver.

Multiply our unnatural and unspiritual rhythm by days, weeks, months, and then stacked-up years and we begin to realize why the soul can feel frayed and worn-out. I say "unnatural and unspiritual" because God had another choice for human beings—a choice to cease. And choosing to cease is choosing to live.

The Different Choice

Soul care in the area of time is God's idea, not ours. Its roots lie in the Ten Commandments, which tell us to observe a span of time "to cease"— the literal meaning of *Sabbath*.

> *Remember the Sabbath day by keeping it holy. Six*
> *days you shall labor and do all your work, but the*
> *seventh day is a Sabbath to the LORD your God.*
> *On it you shall not do any work, neither you, nor*
> *your son or daughter, nor your manservant or*
> *maidservant, nor your animals, nor the alien within*

your gates. For in six days the LORD made the heavens
and the earth, the sea, and all that is in them, but he
rested on the seventh day. Therefore the LORD blessed
the Sabbath day and made it holy. (Ex. 20:8–11)[1]

Through Sabbath keeping, we realize that life is not up to us
and never was intended to be. Sabbath is humanity's reminder, every
seven days, that through resting, ceasing, and unyoking ourselves
from the world and work, we gain something that we cannot have by
working harder. A Sabbath mood is created, which soothes the soul
and sustains our lives when we cease, stop, and enjoy!

I have no desire to tell anyone exactly when and how they must
keep the Sabbath. But what I *am* saying is everyone needs a Sabbath
if they want a soul that can recover from the violence of this world.
Each of us needs a span of time to cease from all the striving that
makes up the rest of our week.

The soulful rhythm initiated by God, modeled by God, and
blessed by God is a six-to-one rhythm. After every six days we are
freed to cease for a span of time equal to a full day. I believe this
is imprinted on our very souls because we were made in the image
of God. God worked for six days then rested on the seventh. Since
we are created in God's image, this God-given rhythm is ours to
live now! It's a six-to-one spiritual rhythm that gives life, sustains
hope, and stirs us to anticipate a day of rest during our other days
that are filled with work. We work for six days; we are to cease for
a twenty-four-hour period of time. Today we are bending this rule
into something that might look like nine-to-one, fourteen-to-one, or
twenty-one–to–one-half. But the soul gets into trouble by ignoring

what God has said was good for us. We cannot sustain the pace by living in a rhythm that is other than what God has modeled and demonstrated for us.

On our Sabbaths, we can be our ordinary selves, resting with our bodies and minds. On our Sabbaths, we might choose not to dress up as we might on working days. We might choose to lounge for hours as we are, in pajamas, T-shirts, and shorts, allowing even our bodies to rest from starch, polyester, and makeup. There is nothing to be "made up" on Sabbath, is there? We can choose to rest in our true selves, with our true and living God, in our true and simple ways, and just be.

Our workweek demands us to be anything but ordinary. We achieve, conquer, make, try, strategize, and plan throughout the week. But there is no one-size-fits-all strategy to Sabbath, only rest—only ceasing from what we've been doing the other six days.

The Meaning of Sabbath

Sabbath is the practice of being available to God by becoming unavailable to the world. That movement—between availability and unavailability—is a dance step to be learned through trial and error. And like anything worth learning, it takes time.

Sabbath is God's invitation to us to come to our senses. Sabbath is a wake-up call offered every seven days to stop, pay attention to what's going on, and reset the trajectory of our lives. Our fast-paced lives are dulling our God-given senses. We listen through little plastic buds; we smell chemical disinfectants; we touch cold, boring keypads; we taste greasy fast foods; and we see only the dust of one another's whereabouts in life. We see a friend's Facebook update but miss the intimacy that a soulful conversation brings when we are truly face-to-face. It could all be so very different for us and Sabbath allows this different kind of a day to be experienced in restoring ways that bring us life and renews us for the week ahead.

Sabbath allows us to "taste and see that the LORD is good" (Ps. 34:8).

Sabbath calls us to cease from the artificial world and cross into the real, living world of creation through nature's delights or the sensual awakenings through amazing flavors enjoyed in a Sabbath meal with friends. As we pull away from technology's ability to dazzle us with a plethora of information at our fingertips, we find we are able to enter the world, where God has been waiting for us all along. We can linger with Him because on this day, on this very blessed day, we do not have to be in such a hurry.

Sabbath stands to remind us every seven days there is no "next." On Sabbath, we do not live with a list of shoulds or things to accomplish. There are no sticky notes reminding us of the chores we must complete. There is nothing to do but to show up and be together. Sabbath is our weekly opportunity to reassess the speed and the trajectory of our lives and make adjustments to stay on course. By not honoring this day of ceasing, we have in fact confessed that we have lost our way, lost a part of our souls that needs to be reclaimed. Sabbath keeping helps us reclaim that which we have indeed lost—a sacred part of our own souls.

And more than that, by Sabbath keeping we are choosing to practice the sovereignty of God. What we say we believe and recite in our creeds is challenged by our lives through the week. Sabbath is an opportunity to cease and trust. We detach from the make-money rush and attach ourselves to a sacred rhythm. We choose the way of the soul over the way of the world.

Listen to the words of one who has attempted to practice the Sabbath.

> *In the eyes of the world, there is no payoff for sitting on the porch. A field full of weeds will not earn anyone's respect. If you want to succeed in this life (whatever your "field" of endeavor), you may spray, you must plow, you must fertilize, you must plant. You must never turn your back. Each year's harvest must be bigger than the last. That is what the earth and her people are for right? Wrong god. In the eyes of the true God, the porch is imperative—not every now and then, but on a regular basis. When the fields are at rest—when shy deer step from the woods to graze the purple clover grown up between last year's tomato plants, and Carolina chickadees hang upside down to pry seeds from the sunflowers that have taken over the vineyard—when the people who belong to this land walk through it with straw hats in their hands instead of hoes to discover that wild blackberries water their mouths as surely as the imported grapes they worked so hard to protect from last year's frost—this is not called "letting things go"; this is called "practicing Sabbath." You have to wonder what makes human beings so resistant to it.[2]*

Resistant to Rest

In some of us there is a compulsion or tendency that resists ceasing. It's a costly tendency. Wayne Muller says it this way in his classic work on the Sabbath: "If we refuse to rest until we are finished, we will never rest until we die. Sabbath dissolves the artificial urgency of our days, because it liberates us from the need to be finished."[3] Sabbath allows us to think about this "artificial urgency" and maddening cadence we are choosing out of habit, ignorance, compulsion, or some other force. Sabbath keeping helps us live in sync with our souls.

There's an old story told by the Cherokee Indians, who lived in my home state of North Carolina. In all its "wisdom," the United States government decided to move the Cherokee nation to the area now known as Oklahoma. A relentless march led by the U.S. Cavalry began, driving the Cherokee people across the rugged mountains and into the flat, dry country where they would live out their days.

As the story goes, the colonel in charge was harsh in his treatment, forcing mothers with nursing infants to walk miles and miles every day. Finally the Cherokee chief could bear it no more and pled passionately with the colonel: "You must let us stop. Our souls need to catch up with our bodies."

You don't have to be a Cherokee Indian to understand the chief's plea. Every corporate worker in a tall downtown office building understands. Every elementary school teacher knows. Every plumber who works long hours and makes himself available on call on holiday weekends to make ends meet understands.

What we seem not to understand, however, is that Sabbath is God's way to help us make ends meet when we feel like we will splinter, fall through the thin ice, and implode if we don't do more. Sabbath reminds us that life is not about our doing *more*. It is about ceasing every six days so that we can truly live. We choose to live when we choose to live in a sustainable rhythm throughout our lives beginning now and here.

Refusing to cease, indeed, is trying to do more than God did. In our sacred text, we read,

> *By the seventh day*
> > *God had finished his work.*
> *On the seventh day*
> > *he rested from all his work.*
> *God blessed the seventh day.*
> > *He made it a Holy Day*
> *Because on that day he rested from his work,*
> > *all the creating God had done. (Gen. 2:2–3 MSG)*

The bottom line is as simple as this: If God, being God, found it necessary and valuable to rest, then who are we to not do the same as the Most High?

Making the Effort to Rest

One church staff asked me to help them begin making some of the choices we are talking about in this book. As I explored the real issues of Sabbath, days off, and time for their own spiritual and physical renewal, it became apparent that the senior pastor felt he could call his staff members on their day off—on their personal day of Sabbath keeping—if he needed something.

One staff member said, "Joe [the senior pastor] will call us to check on how many people came to an event, to make sure we knew that a deacon's wife was in the hospital, or even to see if the alarm system had been properly set because he didn't want to be called in the middle of the night."

In trying to foster a sense of Sabbath keeping and honoring one another, the staff, including the senior pastor, agreed not to call one another on their days off. This seemingly small new agreement brought smiles to their faces and joy to their hearts. *Just think: I can actually be off now and not wonder if I might get a call!* For this staff, not always being on brought new life and hope.

We read in Hebrews, "There remains, then, a Sabbath-rest for the people of God; for anyone who enters God's rest also rests from his own work, just as God did from his. Let us, therefore, make every effort to enter that rest, so that no one will fall by following their example of disobedience" (4:9–11). Here we see that keeping the Sabbath has a paradoxical element to it. We are to "make every effort"—which means exercising some energy, if not work—to actually be able to cease from our work altogether.

For some of us, ceasing won't just happen without some type of commitment or deliberate action (like shutting down the computer or not doing something you could do on another, less holy day). We need to be intentional about it. This is the movement that is birthed in the place of desire where we say, "I *want* this. I *long* for this in my life."

Self-Preservation

Sabbath is God's way of protecting us from ourselves. Left to our own, we will burn out, wear out, and implode. We will live life tired. We will burn the candle at both ends and try and try to make it happen. We will also call this exhausted life the abundant life. There's something very wrong with this! Every seven days we are protected from our own compulsions, addictions, and unhealthy choices.

Because I have my office at home, I'm always faced with a war within me—a fierce civil war of the soul and mind—to cease from using my computer on Sabbath, answering a few more e-mails, writing that one letter that's been hanging over my head, or contacting our donors. I actually believe that if I do more, then something better will happen to me. I think I actually do hear my computer whispering to me, "Come to me. Sit with me and I'll give you the meaning of your life."

Sabbath offers me the choice to choose which voice I will listen to: the one that enslaves me and compels me to do more or the voice that promises me life—real life.

In my own attempts to cease more, I'm now turning my computer off to let even it rest as God says the soil, the vineyard, and crop gathering—everything and everyone—should have a time of ceasing. Ceasing from technology for a day is one step you may want to consider in practicing the Sabbath.

Recently I was teaching a college class on Sabbath keeping. All the students were avid fans of Facebook, instant messaging, Twitter, and texting. I was surprised, however, when I asked them how they could begin to practice Sabbath.

One young woman said, "I feel like a slave to my phone. I know what I can do. On my Sabbath, I'll change the voice mail on my phone to say, 'Hi, this is Cori. It's the Sabbath, and I'm not going to be able to return your call until tomorrow. Talk to you then.'" I smiled as other students nodded in agreement.

One student went on to say, "Sunday phone calls with my parents are always so stressful. They are always asking about my grades and my money. I think I'll ask them if we can talk on another day rather than my Sabbath." Sabbath-keeping allows us to be creative in terms of what and who we might need to "cease from."

There are many ways we can choose to cease, all of them lifesavers. Sabbath protects us from self-destructing by doing too much.

Intimacy Recovered

Sabbath is also a time for us to remember, recall, and be mindful of the people who mean the most to us. Life-giving people are the ones we want to be with on our Sabbath days. On the other days we give and give, but on our Sabbath we receive what we most need!

Imagine every seven days a father turns to his daughter and she gets to see his face—his eyes and not just the back of his head as he leaves for another appointment.

Imagine on this day—this very special, God-ordained day—there is one meal during which the family can sit without the fear of someone rushing off.

Imagine on this day a couple lying down together for a nap, turning to each other in rest rather than fatigue, and expressing their souls' longings to each other in passionate slowness rather than a quick act.

Imagine two friends meeting for a long stroll, then sipping tea under a shaded oak tree while telling each other what their hearts want to say.

The heart needs such times of pause and ceasing to be able to speak the deep things of the soul. Sabbath allows the heart to be primed by extended times of quiet rest that allow feelings, desires, and longings to surface. Most of us just can't start talking when the buzzer rings—at least I cannot. When I meet someone for lunch, it is hard, between the waiter taking my order and the noise of the next table, to shift to talk about what I might really need to say or hear. I need some warm-up time.

The Jewish Talmud (the commentary on the Old Testament Scriptures) encourages men to be sexually intimate with their wives on the Sabbath. The Sabbath was a day for the man to enjoy his wife and the woman to receive her man in soulful "love making" through sexual intimacy. Through a lingering time of togetherness and becoming one—united, naked, and unashamed once more— there is an unspeakable fulfillment in the soul; a husband and wife can enjoy pleasure and nourish intimacy. It is more than the act of sex. It is ceasing from acting, being as real as two souls can be.

For Gwen and I, Sabbath talks are some of our deepest and most honest conversations. Each of us knows that the other will not reach for the cell phone, should it ring, for it and the computer have been turned off on this day. For this day—and only for this day—I am fully and totally available to listen, to hear her, to look at her differently than I would look at her on a Tuesday between appointments. She has told me she needs this kind of focus from me, and Sabbath offers me the choice to focus on her and the other life-giving people in my life.

Rest for the Soul Weary

In our harried world, *rest* often seems like a four-letter word. But it's a sacred, God-breathed, God-modeled, God-blessed four-letter word.

Something happens on a day of rest that does not—cannot—happen in or through another day of sheer work. Through rest the soul is allowed to rev down from the high-powered and sometimes inhuman, if not insane, ways we are living the rest of the week. On Sabbath we embrace our humanity. We remind ourselves that we need to slow down and rest. Our minds need to settle. The stirred soul needs to find its anchor in the midst of a turbulent week.

Sabbath rest is a period of inactivity leading to tranquility. It is a *selah*, or pause, in the midst of life where we linger slowly. Sabbath is a breath to offer the mind, heart, and soul of human beings a chance to receive surpassing experiences of love, peace, and God Himself.

On some Sabbaths Gwen and I agree not to talk about certain people, for it feels like work to talk about them. We agree not to enter into dialogue about projects we are working on together. We do not talk about our ministry, our upcoming week—for that stirs the heart in all the wrong ways. We do not talk about certain themes, wounds, or past mistakes in our own relationship. On these Sabbaths, and because of our own needs, we agree not to "go there" in certain topics that always seem to dredge up dark feelings of anger, resentment, or bewilderment—even consternation—between us.

No, Sabbath is a day to cease from anything that is not life-giving. It is our one day to do what will bring us life, and what does not bring us life—we will leave it to the other days.

If Sabbath, Then Joy

The Jewish prophet Isaiah was the messenger for the very mouth of God when he told us,

> *"If you watch your step on the Sabbath*
> *and don't use my holy day for personal advantage,*
> *If you treat the Sabbath as a day of joy,*
> *God's holy day as a celebration,*
> *If you honor it by refusing 'business as usual,'*
> *making money, running here and there—*
> *Then you'll be free to enjoy God!*
> *Oh, I'll make you ride high and soar above it all.*
> *I'll make you feast on the inheritance of your ancestor Jacob."*
> *Yes! God says so!* (Isa. 58:13–14 MSG)

What's important to note in Isaiah's passionate voice are the dots to connect: Sabbath-keeping and joy are directly related. Did you catch the "if … then" language? *If* we keep the Sabbath, treat it with joy, and honor it as a different day, *then* our benefit is huge. We're told we can actually enjoy God! If we are lacking in joy, we may have violated the rhythm of life. The rhythm of our lives and the joy in our souls are directly related.

Keeping the Sabbath is God's way of sustaining joy in our hearts on the long journey home to heaven. Without it, drudgery is sure, work becomes slavery, and life is nothing more than endurance.

Choosing to honor and keep the Sabbath is a choice to care for our souls. Each time we cease, we take off the yoke of the illusion that it's up to us to make it happen. We are offered this privilege every seven days. Since we are created in the image of God, and since God initiated Sabbath out of His own desire and longing to rest, our Sabbath-keeping is our attempt to live true to ourselves—true to our divine image—true to the way we were created to live. *Selah!*

■ ■ ■ ■ ■

Questions for Reflection

1. Read an overview of the Biblical texts on Sabbath:
   Genesis 2:2; Exodus 31:12–13; Isaiah 58:13–14,
   and Hebrew 4:9–11. Describe what a life-giving
   Sabbath looks like to you. What would you do?
   What would you not do?

2. What kinds of things can you implement on your
   Sabbath to help make this day significant (e.g.,
   light a Sabbath candle, enjoy a meal with friends,
   go on a walk or hike, take a nap, read the Bible as
   a family)?

3. What are the particular challenges you face when
   considering a day of ceasing? Try to think through
   whether these challenges are real or perceived.
   How can you experiment, negotiate, and attempt
   Sabbath-keeping for the next month? Six months?

4. Sabbath keeping is intended to be a "delight," not
   a rule. What needs to happen in your life to keep
   this rhythm from spiraling into legalism?

Notes

1 I find it interesting that the fourth commandment, on the Sabbath, is longer than any of the other nine—offering us the most explanation as to its importance. We're told not to murder in four simple words: "You shall not murder" (Ex. 20:13). But the commandment on Sabbath keeping is much longer. Is this because the wrongness of taking another life is easier to understand than what happens when we violate our souls by working too much?

2 Barbara Brown Taylor, *An Altar in the World: A Geography of Faith* (New York: Harper-Collins, 2009), 133–134.

3 Wayne Muller, *Sabbath: Restoring the Sacred Rhythm of Rest* (New York: Bantam, 1999), 83.

7

Soul Identity

Choosing to Become the Real You

If I find Him, I will find myself, and if
I find my true self, I will find Him.
—*Thomas Merton*

Body and soul, I am marvelously made!
I worship in adoration—what a creation!
—*Psalm 139:14 MSG*

I am often not who I really am.

Image management. It's what we call it when we expend energy, resources, time, and thought in trying to control an image of something, quite often ourselves. Some people hire a public-relations specialist to help them develop the image they want to project. But all of us can try to be our own image management agents by trying to portray to others that we are someone else, someone better or different from who we are really are.

My wife loves to wear an old, threadbare T-shirt that says, "Masquerading as a normal person is exhausting." It's her tongue-in-cheek way of saying, "Love me as I am, even with all of my quirks and flaws." Wearing the shirt is her expression of her desire to be accepted for who she really is.

Choosing to become who we are is one of the most important choices we can make in life. When we choose to be ourselves, we honor God's intent with us. We recognize a holy purpose in our formation. Life becomes an unfolding of our souls that is marked by truth and transformation.

Danish philosopher Søren Kierkegaard prayed a wonderful prayer I've adopted for myself: "And now, Lord, with your help, I shall become myself." There is no self-discovery that happens apart from God. Whether it is through His behind-the-scenes work or the unlikely "burning bushes" of the twenty-first century, it seems God is passionate about our knowing what He already knows about us. Becoming our true selves is a journey of transformation as we learn to give up all the false selves we have tried to be and accept ourselves—with glory and ruin inside.

Saint You

"For me to be a saint means to be myself. Therefore the problem of sanctity and salvation is in fact the problem of finding out who I am and discovering my true self." These are the words of the Trappist monk Thomas Merton, which he wrote while secluded in a monastery in Kentucky, seeking to live his life as a contemplative.[1] His words might sound like navel-gazing—the likes of which you might have little time for. But for Merton, true salvation was far more than being saved from sin. It included being saved from the many false selves he was confronted with even as a monk.

For us, experiencing a deep salvation is necessary due to the world we are living in, a world so taken with airbrushed images of beautiful people, celebrity-status seekers, and social networking that seems more the norm now than the exception. Being saintly while being true to who we really are is our own pilgrimage, though most of us will never see the inside of a monk's cell. We can try to be many people other than who we really are, thus falsifying God's creative work in our own unique and marvelously made souls.

I can try to give you the impression that I am more holy than you, more athletic than the flatfooted runner at the gym, more carb conscious than my overweight neighbor, a more involved parent than the people with the unruly child who sit in front of me at church. The list of what I might want to make others believe about me is endless. The false self clings to this word "more" as a way of making you feel "less" than me.

Spiritual writers down through the ages have spoken about what we call the true self. The journey of life is about taking off our masks and letting our true faces shine forth. It's precisely there, with our uncovered and un-made-up faces, that we stand in great need of soul care. We can live such lies, convincing others and even ourselves that we are more of this or more of that than we actually are. If I am to care for my own soul, then I have to accept myself as I truly am. It is about debunking lies like these:

- "I am what I do." My significance is based on a status job or action I have performed.
- "I am what I have." My significance is based on my accumulation of diplomas and degrees, stock, and square footage.

- "I am what other people think of me." My significance
  is based on others' impressions of me and the energy
  I expend to improve my standing, whether it is true
  or not.

These illusions of ourselves create masks that we begin to wear
early in life. Some of us hide behind the masks for a long time, thinking that no one could ever really love the true us. I love these opening
lines: "Why am I afraid to tell you who I am? I'm afraid to tell you who
I am because you may not like who I am and who I am is all I've got."[2]

Pause for a moment and think about your life right now. What
does your life tell you about yourself—your true soul? Have twisted
lies found a place within you so that you do not believe the truth
about yourself any longer? Becoming your true self may mean
debunking the lies you have come to believe about yourself and
embracing the truth about who you really are—the beloved of God
who is fearfully and wonderfully made!

Making the Choice

An old Hasidic story reveals our need to embrace our true selves. A
disciple named Zusya came to a wise spiritual father seeking advice.
Zusya found himself struggling because he was constantly comparing
himself to others and seeking to be more like them. The old teacher
said, "Zusya, in the coming world, they will not ask you: 'Why were
you not like Moses?' or 'Why were you not like Elijah?' They will ask
you, 'Why were you not like Zusya?'"[3] Zusya had something to learn
about himself. We do too!

The constant comparison of ourselves to each other, the insatiable longings to be someone other than who we truly are, the feelings of shame in not measuring up to someone else's standards—all of these and more are threats to our souls. These fears make the soul shy. And a shy soul never ventures out into the open for fear of its life.

As I drive through the mountain pass to our retreat center, I go by a vast field that is grassy in the summer and snowbound in the winter. I can see thousands of acres where elk come to the edge of the blue spruce, fir, and aspen forest to graze on the pastures. Often, when I drive by, I slow down and spot them hanging on the edge of the forest. I wonder if they're thinking, *Should I come out into the lush green grass and eat what I see is good? If I do, someone might shoot me.*

Does it take courage for the mighty elk to be an elk there in the forest? How do strength and shyness both reside in the meat and muscle, blood and brains of the elk? I don't know these answers. But I know human souls who are very much like the beautiful Colorado elk. Standing proud in the forested trees but timid about being exposed and vulnerable in the open.[4]

Yet every soul, no matter how shy or how filled with ruin, has glory within. Every soul is an image bearer to God, the great Creator, who envisioned each one of us before the mountains and fields were ever formed. Author Ingrid Trobisch reminds us, "God was himself an unwanted child … an embarrassment to his parents, unexpected, and unplanned…. And still, there has never been a child more wanted, more loved by God and never a person who became a greater blessing to more people than Jesus."[5] When Jesus was called "the Beloved," everything changed. His true work began. He gave himself willingly to those who would hear him and he freely laid down his life for us. When we own our beloved-ness and accept our true selves, everything changes for us as well.

Paul reminds the Christ followers at Ephesus of this fact when he writes, "Long before he [God] laid down earth's foundations, he had us in mind, had settled on us as the focus of his love, to be made whole and holy by his love. Long, long ago he decided to adopt us into his family through Jesus Christ. (What pleasure he took in planning this!)" (Eph. 1:4–5 MSG).

How God did this is not the focus of this book, but *that* God did it is. Before the world even existed, God was thinking about our souls—thinking about what distinct markings we would receive, envisioning us physically, emotionally, mentally. He thought us up, and with power no one can ever conceive, our souls were given life. God wants us whether anyone else does or not. And there are no two souls alike—each one bears a certain distinction, a certain aspect of God. When you think about it, this fact alone should motivate us to want to treat one another a little better, be kinder, handle each other with care, and love deeply because of the glory within us.

What I notice today, though, is that there is far more talk about our ruin than about our glory. I believe this should change. When I see a gifted dancer, read a poem by an inspired poet, see a building crafted with the hands of a humble builder, read a book by an amazing author, sit through an eye-opening lecture by a professor, recognize that I am protected in my own country by courageous soldiers, eat the food of inspired cooks, enjoy a vase of flowers arranged by a gifted decorator—I marvel at who really made this possible. I think about the person behind the soul who inspired this dish, this poem, this chair, this clay pot, and then I am led into worship.

Albert Hasse explains it this way: "We have lost our true selves and have gone on a wild-goose chase after false attractions that drive us into a pigpen in a foreign land. We need to come back home and be the people God created us to be."[6]

Here's the truth for us: We can choose to become our true selves. We can decide to relax in our own God-given skins and sink into our God-formed souls. We can accept that we are both sinner and saint, comprised of both glory and ruin.

Finding the Real You

Within each of us there is a civil war raging, and it's not just about whether to sin or to follow God's will. It is a battle to be our true selves or live in a guise of pseudo-reality, not being who we are but living life from a false self. We can cover up who we are by our professions, roles, makeup, and clothes. But this is just a sad attempt to hide what we do not yet know, have not accepted, and are unwilling to be for many reasons.

James Martin writes about this in his book *Becoming Who You Are*. Martin confesses of himself, "The self that I had long presented to others—the person interested in climbing the corporate ladder, in always being clever and hip, in knowing how to order the best wines, in attending the hottest parties, and in getting into the hippest clubs, in never doubting my place in the world, in always being, in a word, cool—that person was unreal. That person was nothing more than a mask I wore. And I knew it."[7]

This was my experience. I tried and tried to be a successful pastor. My mother spoke to me about one church being a stepping-stone to the next and always larger church. If I were to be "successful" in ministry, I would need to measure my success by the size of my congregation. That message got mixed up with another one that said, "Perform well and you'll be the beloved of God. Until you do more, you're really not."

Richard Rohr has told us, "Our false self is who we *think* we are. It is our mental self-image and social agreement, which most people spend their whole lives living up to—or down to."[8]

Fueling the false self requires tremendous energy. The constant comparison, the hunger for more, the drive to be the most gifted or most beautiful or most successful can become insane. This effort becomes all-encompassing and consuming.

The soul of the person who lives from his false self always needs something more, someone more impressive, someone more powerful to reinforce his false identity. For me, crowds, budgets, and programs became like an addictive drug that falsely fueled my soul. External voices clamored to tell me who I was, who I was supposed to be. I lived to please those voices for many years, and I see the same thing happening in the lives of many people around me. I had to come to a point where I could hear, trust, and receive the truth about my own identity as being the beloved of God. The love of God had to become personal and specific to me. It was not enough to simply believe "For God so loved the world…." I had to come to the point in my life where I believed, with all my soul, that God loved me—Steve! Until we reach this intersection on the journey of life, God's love and the search for our own significance will be elusive and fleeting. We will not relax in our own skins. Rather, we will always be trying to be someone else or something more than God fashioned us to be.

My own journey to become my true self meant trying on

clothes—vocationally speaking—that were never me, not made for me to wear, to please my parents. I wore them anyway. But since then my journey has involved taking off the suit and wearing shorts. It has meant leaving the crowds and finding the few. It has meant giving up power and accepting brokenness as true strength. It means not working in offices that are paneled and lacquered but working in a renovated barn at our retreat center that is hidden away from a city.

I visited a friend in her corporate building. Tami's office was spacious, with huge windows looking toward the mountains. It was adorned with plaques, trophies, and framed diplomas she had earned. This was no cubicle, to be sure.

But when the door shut behind me, Tami must have seen my eyes darting around and taking in all of her accumulated accolades. She put her face in her hands and cried, "This is not me. All of this is a lie." She paused, regained her composure, and said, "Don't get me wrong. I'm glad to have achieved this kind of success. But all I want to do with my life is to help people who are suffering. That's what I was made to do."

Tami was headed in the wrong direction. Becoming her true self would mean leaving that world for another world where she felt she could really make a difference. And indeed, after some discussions, Tami did leave her world and join forces with a nonprofit organization through which she helped provide healthy drinking water to remote villages in Africa.

It's Never Too Late to Become Who You Really Are

Author Susan Howatch said, "We are not here simply to exist. We are here to become." What we are to become is our true selves—the exact people God intended for us to be and to become! This is why I love the potter metaphor offered us in the Bible to describe the activity of God and our own spiritual formations. In this image we learn many important things about ourselves. Among the most important lessons is this: The potter's wheel goes around many times. We don't just get one chance to get it right; we get many. Every day, every month, every new job, every new relationship offers us the opportunity to become who we really are. Each passing of the wheel allows the potter to pinch here, squeeze there, bring this up, or push that down.

It's a comfort to realize our claylike states and see that God is the potter after all.

Knowing Self, Knowing God

The voices of church leaders down through the centuries unite in a call for us to enter into times of rigorous self-examination and to know and honor who we truly are. This self-knowledge goes hand in hand with knowing God. Consider this sampling:

- Clement of Alexandria: "If one knows himself, he will know God."
- Augustine: "Grant, Lord, that I may know myself that I may know thee."
- Thomas à Kempis: "A humble self-knowledge is a surer way to God than a search after deep learning."
- John Calvin: "Nearly all wisdom, that is to say, true and sound wisdom, consist of two parts: knowledge of God and knowledge of self."
- René Descartes: "I hold that all those to whom God

has given the use or reason are bound to employ it
in the effort to know him and to know themselves."

Most who have gone before us agree: Knowing our true selves
helps us know the God who really is. Until we plumb the depths to
discover who we are, we can never build a foundation from which
to truly know God. This journey of knowing ourselves necessitates a
slow, steady knowing of God that continues throughout life.

Who am I, really? Asking this question honors your soul and your
Creator. By sitting with this question, you accept the fact that you
are indeed "fearfully and wonderfully made" (Ps. 139:14). Most of
us have not taken the time to wander into our wonder, explore our
claylike souls, survey how God made each of us into a "marvel of
conception" (Job 10:9 MSG). But each of us should. Our marvel of
conception, our fearfully and wonderfully made souls are unique—
never to be repeated, never before made. As "only begotten" as Jesus
was described—we are too!

I believe Thomas Merton has said it best: "There is only one
problem on which all my existence, my peace and my happiness
depend; to discover myself in discovering God. If I find him I will
find myself and if I find my true self I will find him."[9]

No journey of self-discovery can begin without God as our companion. By encountering God, Isaiah encountered himself. As we get
to know God, we get to know ourselves. When Isaiah had the vision of
God being holy, righteous, and filled with glory in the temple, he not
only saw a vision of God as He truly is, he also saw himself. He said,
"Woe to me! … For I am a man of unclean lips" (Isa. 6:5). It was his own
realization of his authentic self before such a God as he had experienced.

To know God—and not just to know *about* God—is fundamental. I only know about the president of our country. I have never met him. I cannot call him a friend or even an acquaintance. Here's the truth: Life both here and in the world to come is linked to knowing God. Jesus said, "This is the real and eternal life: that they *know you*, the one and only true God, and Jesus Christ, whom you sent" (John 17:3 MSG). Life is about knowing God, which leads to knowing our true selves.

When we choose to know God, we also choose to learn about ourselves—and we might find that we didn't wish to know some of that knowledge at all. Seeing our own selfishness, pride, jealousy, deep-rooted anger, and unspeakable shame is never a fun experience. We must view and deal with the ruin before we can make it to glory on the transformational journey of becoming who we really are.

The Beloved of God

During a layover in Toronto, Canada, my wife and I decided to browse a bookstore. The author in me came out, and I couldn't help checking to see if this bookstore carried any of my published books. Upon seeing one of them, I smiled and held it up to show my wife.

Her response? It wasn't what I expected. She said, "Now do you feel like you are the beloved?"

She caught me. I needed public affirmation to feel valuable. My smile and holding up of the book came from some sort of private, secret, and even soul-sick notion of who I was.

Called "my Beloved" at his transfiguration (Matt. 12:18 NLT), Jesus was told who He really was: the delight of the Father. In knowing His true identity, Jesus was able to love others, to give of Himself completely, and even to lay down His life for others. But remarkably, you and I have the same identity. We are not the Son of God in the same sense Jesus is, but we are God's children by adoption, and we, too, are His beloved. Our identity is set. Paul tells us plainly, "Now you are no longer a slave but God's own child. And since you are his child, God has made you his heir" (Gal. 4:7 NLT).

Until we know this core truth for ourselves—that you and I are the beloved of God—we will never experience a healthy soul. We will always be demanding love, using our own power to prove that we are loved, or feeling so unlovable that we are miserable.

Henri Nouwen reminds us, "The greatest trap in our lives is not success, popularity or power but self-rejection." We reject ourselves when we do not believe who we really are. We choose to believe lies about our identity rather than embrace our core truth—that each of us is the beloved of God just like Jesus was. Nouwen goes on to say, "Self-rejection is the greatest enemy of the spiritual life because it contradicts the sacred voice that calls us 'Beloved.'"[10]

Claiming our true identity as the beloved of God is vitally important to having a healthy soul. Until we know this truth for ourselves, we will live in unhealthy ways, chasing anything or anyone that can make us feel loved or who promises to love us. This is why it is correct to say that we *are* the beloved and that we are *becoming* the beloved. We are the beloved as the sons and daughters of God. We become the beloved every time we choose to believe who we are. Here is Nouwen again: "Becoming the Beloved is pulling the truth revealed to me from above down into the ordinariness of what I am, in fact, think of, talking about and doing from hour to hour."[11]

The journey of becoming the beloved is the journey of our lives. It is the quest of our souls. Our beloved-ness is validated, affirmed, and celebrated when we do not close our ears to the voice of God and others speaking into us about who we really are.

We become the beloved every time we rest in who we are apart from what we do, have done, or will do in life. Our beloved-ness does not depend upon accomplishment, goals achieved, or quotas met. Our beloved-ness does not depend upon us at all. Our belovedness depends upon the fact that God says we are lovable—worthy of His love, attention, care, and provision for us. That's it.

The Benefits of Being Me

Caring for your soul means honoring your true identity. When you honor something you protect it, guard it, value it, and care for it. To care for the real you involves the same actions. Recognizing that you are a person of infinite worth simply entails saying, "I matter to God." This thought alone can assuage some of your deepest feelings of aloneness. Knowing that you are the beloved means that you are not alone in this world. You are connected to a sacred family of other beloved sons and daughters whom God loves deeply.

Becoming your true self fosters a deep sense of peace and contentment within your soul. You don't have to strive, yearn, and try to be someone else. You are enough. Hair, complexion, color, physical capabilities as well as limitations are all a part of a sacred design making you an image bearer of God. What you like least about yourself may in some deep way show a God of compassion, creativity, and care at work in your formation. In accepting this, there is great peace.

We are both whole and holy when we become our true selves. Without this, we remain a fraction of who God had in mind, a part—but not the whole—of our true identity. We become holy—a *saint*, as Merton reminds us—when we rest in who we are, knowing that who we are is who God made us to be. No more. No less.

Becoming who we were meant to be is the primary way of knowing the God who really is. By accepting ourselves, we learn to accept a God who is loving, gracious, creative, able to forgive, and willing to extend mercy—all attributes the soul craves to be healthy, free, and alive. Our illusions about God are debunked and the truth of who God really is, not who we have imagined Him to be, allows us to fully worship with renewed hearts and expectant souls capable of spiritual intimacy and true contemplation.

■ ■ ■ ■ ■

Questions for Reflection

1. Read Psalm 139:1–16. As you read David's words, make his words your own. What words or phrases catch your attention?

2. Make an acrostic of your first, middle, and last name. Beside each letter, write a quality or characteristic that you believe describes yourself.

3. Do you feel it's easier to own your ruin than to own your glory? Why or why not?

4. There are many people trying to become their true
   selves apart from God. How would you describe
   what they're doing? How does a follower of Jesus
   Christ become his true self? What do we need to
   do? What do you need to do?

5. The author states three commonly held lies that
   people tend to believe about themselves: "I am
   what I do," "I am what I have," and "I am what other
   people think about me." Which one of these lies
   do you seem to struggle with the most?

Notes

1 These words first appeared in Thomas Merton's book *New Seeds of Contemplation* (New York: New Directions, 2007).
2 John Powell, *Why Am I Afraid to Tell You Who I Am?* (Allen, TX: Thomas More, 1995).
3 As told by Parker Palmer in *Let Your Life Speak: Listening for the Voice of Vocation* (San Francisco, CA: Jossey-Bass, 1999), 11.
4 I am grateful to Parker Palmer for his work on the shy soul in his book *Hidden Wholeness* (San Francisco, CA: Josey-Bass, 2009).
5 Walter Trobish, *Love Yourself* (Downers Grove, IL: InterVarsity, 1969), 19.
6 Albert Hasse, *Coming Home to Your True Self* (Downers Grove, IL: InterVarsity Press, 2008), 12.
7 James Martin, *Becoming Who You Are: Insights on the True Self from Thomas Merton and Other Saints* (Mahwah, NJ: Hidden Springs, 2005), 19.
8 Used by James Martin in *Becoming Who You Are: Insights of the True Self from Thomas Merton and Other Saints,* (Mahwah, NJ: Hidden Springs, 2006), 20.
9 Thomas Merton, *New Seeds of Contemplation* (New York: New Directions, 2007), 36.
10 Henri Nouwen, *Life of the Beloved: Spiritual Living in a Secular World* (New York: Crossroads Publishing Company, 2002), 28.
11 Ibid., 39.

8

Soul Vocation

Choosing What to Do in Life

"The kind of work God usually calls
you to is the kind of work (a) that
you need most to do and (b) that the
world most needs to have done....
The place God calls you to is the
place where your deep gladness and
the world's deep hunger meet."
— *Frederick Buechner*

"Whatever may be your task, work at it
heartily (from the soul), as [something
done] for the Lord and not for men."
— *Colossians 3:23 AB*

You may think it odd that a book about caring for your soul would
explore your work. But think about it: You spend more time at work
than you spend any other place in life. If work's not going well, life's
probably not going well. About 70 percent of people are unhappy in
their current employment due to work-related stress. Whether you

work forty or sixty hours a week or more, your workplace is where much of your waking time is spent. Good work that brings fulfillment, challenge, contribution, and continued motivation is what we want in life. That's no secret.

Vocational issues become central to our thinking about caring for our souls. No discussion about soul care that is legitimate can *only* speak of prayer, solitude, and Bible reading. Today, when there is so much discussion and people in vocational plight, we need to practice "vocation care." As we care for our vocations, we in turn deeply care for the soul.

Before we continue, I'd ask that we pause a moment. I need to voice this. I recently spent three weeks in a developing country where work choices are few and the demands to simply survive each and every day are great. It would seem absurd to ask a person in this country, "What is God calling you to do with you life?"

You and I are privileged to live in a country in which citizens have such choices. True, these choices may not be easy for us to make and at times may be confusing for us. However, we still need to humble ourselves, admit our fortunate place in this world, and give thanks that we have such choices to make when the majority of the world's people have so few. With this fortunate status comes a responsibility for us to own. Jesus' words—"to whom much is given, from him much will be required"(Luke 12:48 NKJV)—cover privileges like this. Making wise choices about what we do with our lives and our abilities becomes a sacred responsibility for us to steward well. Maybe we should stop and consider well the responsibility and stewardship that comes from living in our particular places on the globe. To do less is simply irresponsible.

Curse and Blessing

One of the curses we received from our spiritual ancestors is the inevitable futility and sometimes senseless efforts in our work. Here is what God said to Adam after his original sin.

> *The very ground is cursed because of you;*
> *getting food from the ground*
> *Will be as painful as having babies is for your wife;*
> *you'll be working in pain all your life long.*
> *The ground will sprout thorns and weeds,*
> *you'll get your food the hard way,*
> *Planting and tilling and harvesting,*
> *sweating in the fields from dawn to dusk,*
> *Until you return to that ground yourself, dead and buried;*
> *you started out as dirt, you'll end up dirt. (Gen. 3:18–19*
> *MSG)*

Frustrating, huh? And it all revolves around this thing called work.

Nevertheless, it's important to note that work was a part of God's design for us all along, not just after the big mess with the apple. Work itself is not the soul killer. Work was never meant to be toxic to our well-being. We're told earlier in Genesis that Adam was put into the garden to work and "take care of it" (2:15). I'm sure this garden was comprised of more than patio tomatoes and one row of squash. It would have required sweat work, mindful attention, physical effort to demonstrate care, and more. God intended to make the garden and humanity flourish; He even intended for

Adam to participate in the ongoing creative process He had initiated. Yet after Adam and Eve were caught red-handed in their fiery
disrespect for God's ways, reaping the rewards of the garden turned
from fruit to futility.

We're still feeling the aftereffects of this futility today. Read
these parts again: "You'll be working in pain all your life long....
You'll get your food the hard way ... sweating ... from dawn to
dusk, until you return to that ground." Ask any hardworking person who puts in a good day's effort at a bank, school, or on the road
and you'll hear the echo of Adam's plight. We lament our work like
no other area of our lives. This is why work must be addressed in
the care of the soul.

So why is it important to talk about vocation and caring for our
souls? The bottom line is this: If we're not doing well in our work,
then we're not doing well in our souls. Fil Anderson, author and
spiritual director, puts it this way.

> *When my identity is enmeshed in my work; when the*
> *measure of my worth is my productivity, monetary*
> *success, or renown; when remaining constantly busy*
> *is the thing I do to feel important or to avoid feelings*
> *of emptiness, then in all likelihood my work is toxic*
> *and hazardous to my health. Whenever I'm looking*
> *for myself or trying to escape myself in my work, I'm*
> *flirting with that horrible dependence or addiction*
> *that is workaholism. One very clear symptom is being*
> *constantly consumed with work, such that, even when*
> *I'm not at work, my mind is working on my work.*

*Whenever this occurs, it's certain that all the things
that I claim matter most in my life are suffering,
relationships, personal health, the perspective needed
to enjoy the little things in life, and being able to rest
in the awareness that my work is an important means
and not an end.[1]*

Our Roles and Our Souls

What we do for a living affects our souls. The stress of the workplace, the crisis that is about to erupt, the hidden desire to do something meaningful with our lives—it's all there within us. Deep inside is a brooding, ever-present question: *What should I do with my life?* Unpack that question and you'll likely find potential blessing or a nagging curse.

In most social settings, after we offer our names to someone, the usual next question is "What do you do?" Then we say it and the conversation goes on from there. "I'm a teacher." "I'm a salesman." "I'm a football coach." "I'm a stay-at-home mom." "I sell insurance."

Our "doing" tends to define us—it puts us in a box and labels us. We can assume a certain role in life and thus come to believe that we are what we do. Our work becomes a label that we wear, though sometimes it doesn't fit us well or honor our true selves.

Author Parker Palmer reminds us, "As we become more obsessed with succeeding, or at least surviving … we lose touch with our souls and disappear into our roles."[2] We live divided. Secret ambitions and unredeemed desires run us tired and on empty in life to pursue, get, have, and hoard, then protect all of our assets until we die.

What do you do? Does your work define you correctly? Is the role you have assumed in life the one you *most* want to live? Are you more than the job you do for a living? Day in and day out we work at whatever it is we do for a living, but is your work really you? Caring for your soul must involve a careful examination of this huge reservoir of possibilities because of work's significance in shaping and affecting your soul the right way or the wrong way.

The chasm between our roles and our souls needs to be bridged. Living a life that feels divided between what we do for a living and who we believe we are can leave an emotional cavern the size of the Grand Canyon. This chasm can grow and expand the place in which a soul can hide—perhaps never being known, discovered, or celebrated for anything other than fulfilling tasks—our jobs! We lose ourselves in our roles, never really knowing who we really are apart from our jobs. We become lost in the chasm and divided inside.

Parker Palmer prompts us further: "The divided life is a wounded life, and the soul keeps calling us to heal the wound. Ignore that call, and we find ourselves trying to numb our pain with an anesthetic of choice, be it substance abuse, overwork, consumerism or mindless media noise."[3]

David, who obviously had to navigate his many roles as poet, king, father, and husband, prayed,

> *Teach me your way, O LORD,*
> *and I will walk in your truth;*
> *give me an undivided heart,*
> *that I may fear your name. (Ps. 86:11)*

David was seeking for his life to come together so he would not be divided about what he really wanted in life.

Our prayer might echo David's: "Lord, unite me so that with body, mind, and soul I will have one heart to live by, one heart to give you glory through the one life I am now living. In my being and my doing, let me be undivided so I can truly live."

I often ask people to sit with this question when contemplating a career change: Does your work resemble who you think you are? For many of us, answering this question can help unlock some doors that have been barred too long.

When I asked Jean this question, she immediately said, "Absolutely. I love color, clothes, and watch fashion trends like a hawk." Jean managed a women's clothing boutique but was restless because she wanted to own a store. She felt that owning the store would bring her a deeper sense of fulfillment. She also talked about a secret passion: She wanted to provide clothing for orphans. As we talked about this, Jean felt a courageous move was in order for her to fulfill her dream for herself and orphans. By owning the store, she would have the power and authority to give a percentage of the profits to a cause she really believed in. Jean developed a business plan, showed it to some friends who championed her, and got the funding she needed to open her own boutique across town.

At a recent retreat, a young man named Eric came up after my talk on choosing the right vocation. Eric wanted me to know that even though he was a mechanical engineer, there was far more to him than his drafting papers and calculators would reveal. He said, "People think that engineers don't have a heart, that we are wired in such a way that we can only think with logic, reason, and in a linear fashion."

I nodded, understanding the popular assessment of his people group.

But then tears welled up in Eric's eyes. Choking back his emotion, he said, "I am a man of great heart and great mind. God has given me both dimensions to work with in life. I just wish someone would recognize that I am more than *just* an engineer."

Eric knew something important about his soul. Though his role was to function in one capacity, his soul was richer, deeper, and filled with heartfelt passion about people's relationships with God.

Do you describe yourself as *just* a teacher, plumber, or salesman? Actor Johnny Depp plays J.M. Barrie in the film *Finding Neverland*. When presented with the word *just*, he responds, "What a horrible, candle-snuffing word. That's like saying, 'He can't climb a mountain, he's *just* a man,' or 'That's not a diamond, it's *just* a rock.'"

No one is *just* anything.

Listening to Your Soul

We move from work becoming just work to *good* work when we know who we really are, what our souls are all about, and what God made us for on this Earth. It is about debunking the lie that says, "I am what I do." It is embracing your soul and accepting yourself *as is* with all your imperfections, blemishes, and wounds—as well as gifts, strengths, and assets! In our retreats I sometimes encourage people to write the words "as is" under their names to remind them that all of us are on this journey of discovering our true selves.

The constant comparison of ourselves to each other, the insatiable longings to be someone other than who we truly are, the feelings of shame for not measuring up to someone else's standards—all of these threaten our souls. Parker Palmer comments, "We arrive in this world with birthright gifts—then we spend the first half our lives abandoning them or letting others disabuse us of them."[4]

Embedded in our souls is the God-given birthright to become who we are, to do what we are called to do—whatever that may be. We partner with God in finding this soulful truth for ourselves. We engage with our work, and we also grow in our understanding that our work is not just a means to an end. In ways that humble, inspire, confound, and validate us, we realize that our work gives glory to God.

True vocation is a much deeper journey than taking a battery of tests, filling in a ranking of your gifting, and reading a computer printout that tells you what you should do with the rest of your life. Knowing your true vocation requires a long look into the soul— that place that is the most *you* apart from any role you can fill in life. It's interesting to note that the word *vocation* is rooted in the Latin word meaning "voice"—an inner voice speaking to us, a sacred voice guiding us and nudging us and speaking to us and in us. From this we can understand that we need to listen to our own callings. It's not just the ordained who are privileged to receive such a call but the teacher who must teach because she can't do anything else but teach. The doctor who must heal because he somehow knows this is what he has to do. The artist, the salesman, the missionary, and the rest of us listen and respond through taking up a chosen vocation. There may be many voices that call us to do something until we listen for ourselves and move in faith to accept this call. Until we do so, we will simply perform tasks rather than partner with God in our vocations.

Noted author and minister Frederick Buechner mentions a startling way to approach this.

> *People often ask, "How do you listen to your life?*
> *How do you get into the habit of doing it? How*
> *do you keep ears cocked and your eye peeled for the*
> *presence of God or the presence of anything else?"*
> *One thing I have said, which I think is true, is to*
> *pay attention to any of those moments in your life*
> *when unexpected tears come in your eyes. You never*
> *know when that may happen, what may trigger*
> *them. Very often I think if you pay attention to those*
> *moments, you realize that something deep beneath*
> *the surface of who you are, something deep beneath*
> *the surface of the world, is trying to speak to you*
> *about who you are.... "You never know what may*
> *cause them. The sight of the Atlantic Ocean can*
> *do it, or a piece of music, or a face you've never*
> *seen before. A pair of somebody's old shoes can do*
> *it. Almost any movie before the great sadness that*
> *came over the world after the Second World War,*
> *a horse cantering across a meadow, the high school*
> *basketball team running out onto the gym floor*
> *at the start of a game. You can never be sure. But*
> *of this you can be sure: whenever you find tears in*
> *your eyes, especially unexpected tears, it is well to*
> *pay the closest attention." They are not only telling*
> *you something about the secret of who you are. More*

often than not, God is speaking to you through them
of the mystery of where you have come from and to
summoning you to where, if your soul is to be saved,
you should go to next.[5]

What moves you? When do you feel passion rise within you that you cannot push down any longer? The beach ball that children play with at the shore will always come up no matter how many kids sit on it or force it under. Passion works this same way. Through the decades of our vocational journeys, we learn to mismanage our passion rather than release it to move us out from stuck places—places where we no longer belong, places that we have outgrown, places that don't breathe life into us and help us stay alive. Yet for many strange reasons, we can push passion down, ignore the voice calling us to move out, take a risk, do this or that.

Years ago, vocational trade schools and technical colleges were established. A these institutions, a person could register for classes, learn a skill, get a job, and move on with life. One track would lead to work as a plumber, another track to becoming an office assistant. A person signing up for such a track might do so on a hunch, through validation of his or her gifting, or out of desperation for a job. The classes were meant to educate, train, and give a person the skills needed to be successful.

True vocation, however, is not something we sign up and acquire the skills for. The word *education* means far more than imparting information for someone to learn. It means to "draw out" of someone what is already there—perhaps latent, dormant, and very much underdeveloped. To educate people about their true vocation means to tap into the reservoir within them that is calling them to become the persons that God has made them to be.

More than filling in the gaps of missing bits of information and techniques, the journey of finding your true vocation is first looking within the soul and surveying what God has already put in you to be who he made you to become. When you find it, it will feel right.

"Oughtness"

Vocation is birthed from what philosopher Henry Bugbee called an ethic of necessity: It's not something we have to do or even should do; it's something we *must* do.

Rainer Maria Rilke gave advice to an aspiring poet that is important to all job-searching people. In his book *Letters to a Young Poet*, Rilke writes,

> You ask whether your verses are good. You ask me.
> You have asked others before. You send them to
> magazines. You compare them with other poems,
> and you are disturbed when certain editors reject
> your efforts. Now … I beg you to give up all that.
> You are looking outward and that above all you
> should not do now. Nobody can counsel and help you,
> nobody. Search for the reason that bids you to write;
> find out whether it is spreading out its roots in the
> deepest places of your heart, acknowledge to yourself
> whether you would have to die if it were denied you
> to write. This above all—ask yourself in the stillest

hour of your night: must I write? Delve into yourself
for a deep answer. And if this should be affirmative,
if you may meet this earnest question with a strong
and simple "I must," then build your life according
to this necessity; your life even in its most indifferent
and slightest hour must be a sign of this urge and a
testimony to it.[6]

Rilke's words seem like good spiritual direction for us regardless of whether our vocation is to be a poet or a plumber. "Search for the reason that bids you" to do what you want to do. "Delve into yourself for a deep answer…. Then build your life according to this necessity."

Work is more than mere work when we realize, *This is what I was made for—this is what I must do.*

Why Did God Make You?

One Christmas vacation our family gathered in our living room near the Christmas tree. I asked my four grown sons, "What kind of work do you think you'd enjoy doing for the rest of your life?" It was a question to stir the pots of their souls and probe them to think about life beyond college.

My son Jordan was then in his senior year of college. He would soon be commissioned as an officer in the United States Army. His words were true for him to say but hard for us to hear. "Dad and Mom, I know why God made me."

He had our full attention. I said, "Why, Jordan? Why did God make you?"

Jordan took a long breath and said, "God made me to be a soldier. I'm going to be in the infantry, and I'm going to be a soldier."

We knew Jordan would be in the armed forces for the next four years to pay the army back for his wonderful education. He had accepted a scholarship that paid for his university education almost in full, but in exchange, he would have to serve for several years in the military. Our hope was that Jordan would get a safe desk job, perhaps sending e-mails for a general.

But Jordan knew what we did not know—and what we did not want to admit about him—namely that he was uniquely built to become a twenty-first-century warrior. From a physical standpoint—chiseled chest, minimal body fat, and a competitive spirit like no one I've encountered—Jordan was suited for this role. He dreamed of becoming an officer in the infantry, going into combat on the front lines. It was his sense of "must."

And in fact, after graduation, Jordan was selected to train to be an army ranger. Only a third of those who try to become an army ranger actually become one due to the rigorous training that a ranger has to successfully complete. But Jordan was right: God made him to be an infantry officer.

Today many people who are my son's age will inevitably have four or five different jobs in their lifetimes. Each job becomes its own "school of the soul" to inform us, teach us, nudge us, and beckon us forward and on to the next—hopefully the right—position. Each job, each position becomes a sort of voice informing us of the next step. So our encouragement is simply this: Our lives' work is really a composite of all the jobs—good and bad, success or failure—that teach us, make us, and shape us for our calling.

Progressive Revelation

Not many of us can say in our early twenties, "I know why God made me." This is a knowledge that most of us come to realize only after years of trying different kinds of work. Taking a job can be like trying on clothes to get the right fit. *That one seems too big. This one is too small.* Try a job for a while and you may realize, *No, that's not me. It's not what I want to do.* For many of us, it's a live, try, and learn process that must be allowed in our vocational journeys.

Our oldest son, Blake, already an army officer, heard Jordan declare his life's vocation to us. When Jordan finished, Blake jumped in and said, "I'm already an army officer, and that's *not* why God made me. I'm in the army because the army would pay for college. I'm thinking about going into the ministry." Blake has a different understanding of his life. His choices are different; his motivations are different from Jordan's; and his life will likely look different, though they come from the same genetic pool.

Most of us are not given work epiphanies through which we know in a split second what we should be doing. Each step of the journey informs the next step. To borrow a theological term, it's called "progressive revelation." Truth grows within us and is validated and confirmed as we move to the next step or place—hopefully to a place that is better lit. Each job informs us that we are getting closer. The next one might just be the fit we've been looking for in our vocational quests. Paying attention to what you learn in each workplace about yourself is as important as fulfilling the certain role that your job demands of you.

Wayne began his career as a sheet-metal worker in a factory. He remained in this job for fifteen years, working his way up to a shift manager. Through a series of events, including a divorce and a move to start his life over, Wayne became a Christian and started attending the church I pastored. He also realized that he wanted something more out of life than cutting sheet metal. He told me that his secret ambition in life was to become a hairstylist.

Wayne's transformational journey resulted in changing his vocation from cutting metal to cutting hair. Now he is one of the most sought-after hairstylists in the city. His vocational journey required him to take the jokes that were hurled at him from his team at the sheet-metal factory, enroll in a program through which he could learn how to become a stylist, and muster up the courage to begin his new career, build his reputation, and eventually open his own business. Each step shed light on the next for Wayne.

What is important to remember in discerning your vocational calling is that there is no cookie-cutter approach for a soul to go into one way and come out the same. Each of us is different, fearfully and wonderfully made, and the calling for our vocational pursuits is also varied. Exploring the fabric of your own soul with a trusted friend, spiritual guide, or mentor can be very helpful in discerning the right choice for you. Doing the deep soul work now is an important part of the journey. Live your questions and pick up unturned stones and look under them for the truth. Macrina Wiederkehr, a Catholic writer, has a beautiful prayer that is funny yet hauntingly true when seeking such knowledge about ourselves. She prays,

O God,
Help me

to believe
the truth about myself
no matter
how beautiful it is![7]

It may be hard for some of you to pray this prayer well. But accepting the truth of this prayer about yourself is key to living the life you were meant to live and doing what you were created to do.

Discerning the truth about ourselves and our callings, combined with our passion, interests, and giftedness, is a coming-together process called convergence. A life in which convergence happens is a life that is stewarded well and lived with great fulfillment, leaving a legacy to be remembered for a long, long time.

Convergence

Vocational convergence occurs when our formal and informal education, on-the-job training, valuable experience, sacred giftedness, skills, and opportunities come together, giving us sight of where we are to head in life.[8] It is not up to us to make or force this coming together. It is God who shapes our time, opens the doors for opportunities, and orchestrates events over time.

Convergence begins to happen in life through decades of working here and there, seeing a door opening (perhaps someone giving us a break—an opportunity that seems too good to be true), and having a sense of divine appointment to something so good that God must be at the root of it all. It usually does not happen quickly. There is much to learn that only years and time can teach us. The soul may have to weather many vocational storms to grow wise and understand this coming together.

It is my opinion—one that isn't substantiated by empirical proof—that convergence does not happen in our twenties when we are starting out in our careers. It does not happen in our thirties, when energy levels are high, motivation is sharp, and drive is steadfast. It may not happen in our forties, when we enter the "midlife crisis."

I see it mostly happening in our fifties and beyond.

In our fifties we have finally earned the right to lift our heads up and say some things that we really are sure of, things that are true, tried, and tested. In our fifties we are becoming the wise ones: We are still able to relate to a younger generation behind us, but we see the end coming into sight. Our days might be spent taking care of aging parents, and we may find ourselves walking away from the freshly dug graves of friends who died much too soon. Yet we still have a resolve to do something—something we sense we were made to do. Passion has been tested in the past, but now it is time for the release of mature passion, not just youthful energy and vigor. Bridled energy is surer, and strength is not diminished by effort.

When a door of opportunity opens, light is shed onto the path, making the next path more visible, less risky. All of the experiences of the past, all of the jobs, all of the bosses that we did not like and the few we did, all of the mentors who helped us—these begin to cheer for us. Or do we just now finally and really hear them and let ourselves move forward? We cannot go back to the younger days. We don't want to. We cannot live the afternoon of our lives as we did the morning. Deep down our souls say, "This is why I was made. I was made for this."

Jeff showed up in my office dressed in his salesman clothes: starched shirt with red tie, navy slacks, and polished leather shoes. But beneath that neat façade was a mess! Jeff felt like his life had become a joke. His story might shed light for some of us.

At his father's urging, Jeff went to a college he really didn't want to attend. He became what his father wanted him to become—a second-generation business owner. He lived this life for a number of years before a gnawing sense of depression and futility rose up within him.

Through our times of talking, Jeff confessed that he really wanted to be a landscaper. His love of dirt, plants, and nature were deep truths—soul truths. When I asked Jeff what he would do if money were no object, he said, "I would want to work in nature, making places of beauty for people to enjoy."

Jeff told me that as a boy, he spent all of his free time planting a flower and vegetable garden for his parents and making money by mowing neighbor's yards. Yet this childhood passion had been replaced by a demanding father's voice, which seemed to replace Jeff's own voice expressing what he really liked—what he really wanted to do. Now, twenty years into his profession, Jeff was willing to rethink everything and go for his dream: to run a landscape service. It would mean giving up a lifestyle he and his wife had enjoyed. But Jeff realized that no lifestyle was worth the discontent he felt inside, and his wife agreed. Jeff found what he *must* do.

When I look back on my vocational journey, I can now see a progressive revelation that was at work within me to help me have a true sense of calling in my life. In some jobs, a few people became significant and major cheerleaders—true soul champions for me to help me better understand myself. Hard experiences in my work offered me valuable lessons I needed to learn about perseverance and endurance. God helps each of us to reframe each experience we have in our work and see the necessary lessons we needed to learn. Oftentimes failing well can teach us more than succeeding badly.

We are living in a challenging work environment. You may not get to work in the job you most want to work in. Your real work might be finding the right job and sometimes a job to simply pay the bills. There is no shame in this. All work is God-work if it is done for God.

Author David Whyte tells us the antidote to exhaustion is not rest, but wholeheartedness. When we are sick and tired of our work, rest and more rest may not really be the answer we need. We may need to find the work that we are called to, created for, and that all of our life has been but preparation for.

Reminiscing on the cold, snowy, winter afternoon US Airways Flight 1549 crashed into the Hudson River in 2009, Captain "Sully" Sullenberger said, "All my life came down to this one moment." He was describing the moment when two flocks of birds flew into the direct flight path of the jet, causing complete engine failure. The captain had to crash-land the plane into the freezing Hudson River. Incredibly, no lives were lost, and the captain is now regarded as a hero. When we can say, "All my life has come down for this ... for you ... for this cause ... for this project," we are living for a greater purpose than self, a greater calling than ego, and a greater sense of fulfillment than money can pay us.

A man who had served as a missionary in Africa for twelve years revealed his soul's new confession when he said, "Steve, I no longer want to worship my work or myself through my work. I want my work to be worship." When our true vocation is offered to God, we are giving God great glory.

May we all see the convergence that God is arranging to give us our true vocation, and let our souls flourish.

■ ■ ■ ■ ■

Questions for Reflection

1. Read Exodus 31:1–11 and explore these questions: How do Bezalel's skill, experience, and passion display themselves? What insights can you learn from Bezalel's vocational journey that can impact your own?

2. As you look back on your vocational journey, how would you say your work has affected your soul?

3. What are some ways your roles have shaped your soul, both positively and negatively?

4. As you read the story about the young poet approaching Rilke, do you have a sense of "mustness" in you right now—something you sense you must be about in regard to your life?

5. How can you trace the author's idea of "progressive revelation" in your life? How does

your own story inform you about any next steps
you should consider?

Notes

1 Fil Anderson in "Work," in *The Transformation of a Man's Heart* (Downers Grove: Inter-
   Varsity Press, 2008), 90.
2 Parker Palmer, *A Hidden Wholeness: The Journey Toward an Undivided Life* (San Francisco,
   CA: Jossey-Bass, 2009), 15.
3 Ibid., 20.
4 Ibid., 12.
5 Frederick Buechner, *Beyond Words: Daily Readings in the ABC's of Faith* (New York: HarperOne, 2004.)
6 Ranier Maria Rilke, *Letters to a Young Poet* (First Vintage Books: Random House, New
   York, 1986), 5–6.
7 Macrina Wiederkehr, *Seasons of Your Heart: Prayers and Reflections* (New York: HarperCollins, 1991), 71.
8 Dr. Robert Clinton coined this use of the term *convergence* for ministry leaders in his book
   The Making of a Leader (Colorado Springs, CO: NavPress, 1988). However, convergence
   is not limited to people in full-time ministry.

9

Soul Address

Choosing to Honor the Body-Soul Connection

He who does good to his own
self is a person of mercy
—*Proverbs 11:17, author's paraphrase*

Our bodies are apt to be
our autobiographies.
—*Frank Gillette Burgess*

I grew up in the South, where the body was not talked about much—although feeding the body was a prominent part of every gathering. I had never heard of a carbohydrate. I never knew about the glycemic index.

Preachers discussed matters of life and death and heaven and hell over blackberry cobblers, warm banana pudding with fluffy meringue, and cheesy squash casseroles with toasted bread topping. Men's breakfasts in my church revolved around waffles dripping with warm maple syrup and piles of butter, plates heaped high with ham biscuits. The fellowship halls of my youth didn't have round tables where people could sit and talk with one another. They had only rows and rows of long rectangle tables, something that could handle the "spread." Funerals were times of comfort with long tables laden with the best food you had ever put into your mouth. Weddings were times to feast. Every time people gathered, there was food.

The church I went to every week as a boy also had a "smoking patio," where the men could gather between Sunday school and "preaching service" and smoke a quick cigarette. I lived in a state where tobacco was the largest cash crop, and no one dared preach against something that supported the church with the tithes and offerings from the sale of cigarettes.

That smoking patio was never questioned, but it's where I was always sure to find my dad—or where I could avoid him if I wanted to sneak out and walk two miles to get a cherry Coke with a friend and then tell my parents how much I liked the sermon I never heard.

And so in my Southern church we talked a lot about taking care of the spirit and very little about taking care of the body. The body was an afterthought, something we needed to tolerate until we got to heaven. What we put into it seemed to have little impact. What we thought of it was of even lesser importance.

For these reasons and many others, it has taken me several decades to realize that God never intended for us to separate the body from the soul. Body care, in fact, is an essential part of soul care. I am just beginning to understand what this means. In the book *Younger Next Year*, authors Chris Crowley and Henry Lodge state the following: "People who report that faith is an important part of their lives have mortality rates a third lower than average. They have lower blood pressures and lower blood sugar levels; spend few days in the hospital; and report substantially high levels of life satisfaction and emotional well-being."[1] Making the connection between our bodies and soul has its own rewards.

Confessions of a Body-Care Beginner

An old story rooted in Jewish tradition reminds us of the connection between our bodies and our souls.

Hillel the Elder was a wise, old rabbi who one day bid farewell to his disciples, who followed him everywhere.

> One disciple asked him, "Rabbi, where are you
>   going?"
> The rabbi replied, "To do a good turn to a guest in
>   my house."
> The disciple replied, "Every day you seem to have a
>   guest."
> To which the rabbi said, "Is not my poor soul a guest
>   in my body?"[2]

Learning to care for our own bodies is a way of being hospitable to the souls that live within us. Our souls, after all, are guests in the physical tent of our skin, bones, and muscles. Yet many of us take better care of our physical homes—the shingles on our rooftops, the quality of our windows, the strength of our walls—than our souls' physical homes.

Now I must admit something to you. I am late in waking up to the significance of my body. As I write this, I am midway through my fifth decade and already I feel the effects of a lifetime of being unaware of my physical self. Food in particular is a drug I've chosen to try to bring solace to my soul.

Over the years I chose to believe the lie that I had to settle for the body I was given. Maybe I even mouthed off a time or two, "It's my DNA. Look at my mother's side of the family, for crying out loud." Maybe I believed the illusion that food could comfort me in ways that God never could.

In recent years, however, I have friends who through their gentleness and kindness are urging me to rethink my body, and my wife is chief among these voices cheering me on. I see now that old age is a possibility for me, and if I get there, I'd like to be healthy and enjoy it. More than that, I want my body to be healthy because I want my soul to be healthy, and God created our bodies, souls, and minds to be healthy or unhealthy together, to work with each other for better or for worse.

Consider this analogy: In most farming communities, farmers place silos side by side. One holds corn, others hold various kinds of grains. For too long I have had a "silo mentality" of life. I, like many of us, have spent most of my life thinking of God in a big silo, with smaller silos next to him, holding "work," "family," "exercise," and other aspects of life.

I am not alone in my silo views. The term "spiritual formation" is an in-vogue way of talking about how God, like a divine potter, shapes us—pressing here, pinching there—to mold us into the desired image. While the evangelical church is embracing this concept more and more, we are not yet embracing the fact that our physical, material, real, tangible flesh and blood needs to be incorporated into our spiritual lives.

Dallas Willard writes that the role of the body in the spiritual life is "probably the least understood aspect of progress in Christlikeness." He goes on to explain why neglecting the body can hurt our spiritual lives.

> *Some may think it strange that [spiritual disciplines] are all bodily behaviors. But it cannot be otherwise. Learning Christlikeness is not passive. It is active engagement with and in God. And we act with our bodies. Moreover, this bodily engagement is what lays the foundation in our bodily members for readiness for holiness, and increasingly removes the readiness to sin.[3]*

I am learning that the soul has no silos. The soul is the place where everything—physical needs, spiritual needs, and intellectual needs—comes together. We are not soulful spirits. We are whole creations that require holistic care in each and every part of our lives.

Becoming Curious

Becoming curious about our souls allows us to become curious about our bodies. Everything is on the table for us to explore: The mystery of sex, the impact of physical disease on our spiritual lives, how physical disabilities may enhance spiritual abilities, how "thorns in the flesh" (an expression Paul uses in 2 Corinthians 12) can strengthen us spiritually. This curiosity will lead us to explore our sexual stories and how they impact our souls. It will lead us to look at parts of ourselves that we simply do not like—maybe even hate. How do our strong feelings about our bodies affect how we think God sees us? If we struggle with self-rejection, self-hatred, and self-disgust, how does this impact our impressionable souls? Knowing more about the complexities of our bodies make us more aware, more humble, more careful about the care of our souls. So rather than accepting the common complaints that we are tired, overweight, or imperfect, let us work out our salvation through learning what it means to honor our bodies.

To understand my spiritual journey, I had to look back at my physical journey. This has given me keen insight and awareness about my own body-soul connection. Food, like many bodily needs, is a great gift. But when I put it in the place of God, it separates me from what I need the most. Food—no matter how creamy, icy, sweet, or salty—cannot care for my soul.

Maybe food is not the temptation for you it is for me. Maybe for you it's stress, smoking, alcohol, lack of sleep, lack of exercise, lack of food, various chemical or emotional dependencies, or a distorted body image; all are factors when we consider how we are caring or not caring well for our bodies.

Of course we all know what is good and bad for our bodies— news articles and doctors remind us often enough of what healthy living looks like. But when we realize that caring for our bodies is a way of caring for our souls, our perspective on "getting in shape" or "getting more rest" changes.

We already know that we should eat less and exercise more. Recently I went to a Weight Watcher's meeting for some encouragement on my own body-care journey. The leader started the session,

"How many of you know that to lose weight you need to eat less, exercise more, and drink more water?" Every hand went up. But just because we know this does not mean we are doing it. Why is this? Why do we keep failing to do what we say we want to do? We need to find a soul connection that will inspire us to work more deeply.

Making a body care commitment to your own soul can be a challenge when you travel and order room service. After all, who's going to know that you order extra french fries and the chocolate ice cream sundae? Making healthy choices and keeping promises and commitments are more important when you make them for your own soul rather than when you make them for someone else.

With all this in mind, consider what actions or inactions of your life are hurting the body God gave you. What thoughts about your body are seeping into the life of your soul? In what ways might you be looking for bodily satisfaction at the expense of soul satisfaction? In what ways are you assuming soul satisfaction can come no matter how you care for your body?

As I'm aging, I'm thinking more about my past—how I got to be the way I am and the many areas of my life that need transformation. You might want to do the same as you consider the relationship between your body and soul. How did others view the body when you were growing up? How did you learn about your sexual self? In what ways did you see the body abused or honored? What did food mean to you growing up? What gave your body comfort?

Even as we ask these questions, we know that we should not give in to the pressures of the world to exalt the body above all else. So how do we honor and care for our bodies in a godly, earthy, but not earthly way? And why does it matter?

Where God Dwells

In her book *An Altar in the World,* Barbara Brown Taylor writes, "Whether you are sick or well, lovely or irregular, there comes a time when it is vitally important for your spiritual health to drop your clothes, look in the mirror, and say, 'Here I am. This is the body-like-no-other that life has shaped. I live here. This is my soul's address.'"[4] Some of us rush by the mirror, too ashamed to look at the sheer miracle of our bodies—no matter what shape we are in. We do not stop and appreciate how our bodies have actually served us and gotten us to where we are right now: a place to make an even better choice.

In Scripture your "soul's address" is referred to as the temple of the Holy Spirit. In other words, your body—whatever shape, size, or appearance—is where God chooses to dwell. This reason alone affirms the importance of our physical beings. Our bodies matter because our sacred soul dwells within our physical body.

God designed us to "offer the parts of our body to him as instruments of righteousness" just as we offer to him our souls (Rom. 6:13). Whatever spiritual disciplines we engage in for the soul affect our bodies. However we treat the body affects the soul. God created them to be inseparable.

Nearly all spiritual disciplines involve some physical response. We kneel. We bow our heads. The ancient discipline of fasting in particular closes the gap of our body and soul connection.[5] Fasting humbles our souls (Ps. 35:13 and Deut. 8:3), helping us practice feasting on God, not just on food.

Spiritual disciplines are often called exercises—perhaps a more appropriate term to help us make the body-soul connection. Paul tells us, "Exercise daily in God—no spiritual flabbiness, please! Workouts in the gymnasium are useful, but a disciplined life in God is far more so, making you fit both today and forever. You can count on this. Take it to heart. This is why we've thrown ourselves into this venture so totally" (1 Tim. 4:7–10 MSG).

"A disciplined life in God" is a life in which we make space for God—even in our bodies. Throughout Scripture we are encouraged to abstain from things that harm the body and involve ourselves in what will help the body—and therefore nourish the soul.

Perhaps people of other religions know the value of involving the whole body in spiritual disciplines more than modern Christians do. When Muslims pray, the whole body moves; they kneel, fall to their faces, rise again. Seven times a day they involve their entire bodies in prayers to Allah. When I travel internationally on airplanes it's not unusual for me to see a Muslim praying in the aisles of the airplane, unashamed of his body's role in praying.

In contrast, most of us know how trying to pray while getting ready to sleep often ends in simply falling asleep. Physical involvement such as kneeling, nodding, dancing, or raising one's arms can help connect the body and soul in simple but life-changing ways.

We're told that David, King of Israel, danced before the Lord. David's worshipful expression of joy seems lost in many churches today, but David had no problem involving his whole body in the act of celebration and worship.

Sometimes when I sit down at church, I become more aware of how tired I am. The week catches up with me. I just want to sit, disengage. But as I'm directed to stand, kneel, or turn around and greet my neighbor, my body wakes up. I start getting involved in the movement of worship. As my body engages, so does my heart and soul.

I also find that walking is a good way to connect my body and soul. I call them "God walks"—times each week when I walk on a trail by my house. As I walk I'm conscious of keeping my heart rate up and my prayers going up as well. God walks have become a therapy for my soul and body.

Danish theologian Søren Kierkegaard said, "Above all, do not lose your desire to walk. Every day I walk myself into a state of well-being and walk away from every illness. I have walked myself into my best thoughts and I know of no thought so burdensome that one cannot walk away from it."[6]

What is important is to find how you can make the body-soul connection in your life. It may come by running, going to the gym, or pilates. An earthly approach to all this ends in the word *shape,* and usually a predetermined, Hollywood-trainer-created shape. Chances are very good it's been airbrushed. A soulful approach, however, is concerned with the word *fit* or *well-being.*

Over one hundred fifty years ago this connection between body and soul spurred a man named George Williams to found the Young Men's Christian Association—known today simply as the YMCA. Read the words from the Y's own documents about their beginnings.

The Young Men's Christian Association was founded in London, England, on June 6, 1844, in response to unhealthy social conditions arising in the big cities at the end of the Industrial Revolution

*(roughly 1750 to 1850). Growth of the railroads
and centralization of commerce and industry
brought many rural young men who needed jobs
into cities like London. They worked 10 to 12 hours
a day, six days a week.*

*Far from home and family, these young men often
lived at the workplace. They slept crowded into
rooms over the company's shop, a location thought
to be safer than London's tenements and streets.
Outside the shop things were bad—open sewers,
pickpockets, thugs, beggars, drunks, lovers for hire
and abandoned children running wild by the
thousands.*[7]

In the United States, evangelical Dwight L. Moody became one
of the YMCA's most ardent supporters and advocates in the mid
1800s. He saw that caring for the body was a way to care for the
souls of men and women. The YMCA and YWCA became major
evangelistic organizations that saw thousands of people experience
salvation both physically and spiritually. Today, the Y continues its
mission to help people live well through the "development of spirit,
mind, and body."

God's Validation of Our Physical Bodies

Our physical bodies received their validation when God became a
human being. Through the incarnation Jesus chose to enter into

the marvel of humanity and be fitted with sinew, muscle, body fat, organs, and a brain. Jesus made the body-soul connection that we need to make today. The physical became spiritual. God chose the body to reveal His true nature—not a cloud, not a building, not a machine—but flesh and blood, hair and knuckles, fingers and toenails.

A tenet of Christianity is the belief that Jesus' body rose to heaven, not just His soul. Jesus asked us to remember His body and blood, and we do every time we take the bread into our mouths and swallow the cup's wine. These earthy tents that house our souls matter even in heaven.

How I treat my body is how I am treating my fearfully made and wonderfully shaped soul. To honor my soul means to honor the body in which my soul dwells. Our bodies are the new "Bethlehem of Jesus," as author and pastor Oswald Chambers reminds us. We are told that Christ is *in* us—He has taken up residence within our bodies. To abuse or neglect the body is to do violence against our souls. When I think of body care in this way, I am motivated to stop hurting what is spiritual.

Spiritually One

Our bodies become the stories of our lives. The wrinkles of worry on our faces show the fault lines of tension, anxiety, and gnawing depression we have experienced. Our scars reveal outer wounds and leave clues of the inner ones—the ones that often go unnoticed and unshared but still store the soul's wear and tear. Our joys of sexual pleasure, intimacy, and oneness reflect our longing to be connected with each other in hallowed and private worship where words fail to express what the body feels. Our bodies, in fact, reveal a significant part of our spiritual formation.

Consider what Paul's words about sex tell us about how the body affects who we are.

> There's more to sex than mere skin on skin. Sex is as much spiritual mystery as physical fact. As written in Scripture, "The two become one." Since we want to become spiritually one with the Master, we must not pursue the kind of sex that avoids commitment and intimacy, leaving us more lonely than ever—the kind of sex that can never "become one." There is a sense in which sexual sins are different from all others. In sexual sin we violate the sacredness of our own bodies, these bodies that were made for God-given and God-modeled love, for "becoming one" with another. Or didn't you realize that your body is a sacred place, the place of the Holy Spirit? ... So let people see God in and through your body. (1 Cor. 6:16–20 MSG)

Here Paul reminds us that bodily acts directly relate to acts of the soul. A physical action can lead us "to become spiritually one with the Master," or it can take us farther away from God, "leaving us more lonely than ever." We also learn that how we treat our bodies can lead others closer to God or farther away. With this understanding, sexual intimacy becomes more than an act. It becomes the ultimate body-soul connection with another body and soul. What power the body has! There really is no such thing as safe sex.

Through God's Eyes

Just as our awareness of God's love affects the life of the soul, it affects the life of the body. The deepest truth about ourselves is that we are the beloved of God. We are also becoming the beloved as we live. Henri Nouwen reminds us that "self rejection is the greatest enemy of the Christian life."[8] Perhaps our journey to accept and care for our bodies reflects the dangers of self-rejection more than any other aspect of the Christian life.

Being disappointed with our bodies is the malaise of our time. Some of us cut, mutilate, harm, and abuse our normal, everyday bodies, while others are obsessed with percentages of body fat, blood levels, and time at the gym. Our fears and disappointments about our bodies can seem overwhelming at times—especially when we are alone with our inner voices of self-rejection. It doesn't have to be this way. No one feels particularly sexy or good after they've battled breast cancer the way my wife did several years ago. No one wants to be a cancer victim. No woman wants to have a hip replacement at age forty-four like my friend Beth did. But such medical challenges offer deeper choices such as: "How am I going to live in light of this new condition? Where is God in this? And what will recovery be like in my soul as well as my body?"

As you know by now, I encourage people who are struggling in their soul to have some quiet time alone every day. People often need coaching in practicing this discipline because the voice of self-condemnation can speak more loudly than God's voice at first. It's hard to enjoy the rewards of silence and solitude when you hear a crowd of voices jeering at you.

Sometimes I ask people to take a journal with them and write down all that they hear in their initial times of silence and solitude. One woman, Cheryl, came back with three pages of single-spaced statements that she heard when trying to be quiet. She read to me what she heard.

- "You are so messed up; you are beyond help."
- "You have had so many sexual partners; you cannot be the beloved of God."
- "You are disqualified."
- "Look at what you did. You had an abortion."
- "You're too fat."
- "You should be ashamed of yourself. Look at what your life has become."

The list goes on.

This exercise reveals the amount of self-rejecting lies we learn to believe about ourselves, God, and others. For Cheryl, debunking these lies meant deconstructing each lie she believes about herself, her body, and what she had done with her body—and replacing those lies with the truth. Others might add voices about sexual or physical abuse, reminders of wounds that affect how they view their bodies every day.

Putting to rest such deep lies requires more than a one-time, fix-it-all solution. Like every aspect of soul care, recognizing, facing, and refuting the lies about our bodies is an ongoing process, one that only the Holy Spirit in us can complete. Choosing to face the lies that we believe frees us to leave our victim status and regain the truth—the only thing that will allow us to live out of our true selves.

Our healing often begins by recognizing the difference between accepting our bodies through God's eyes and striving for the approval of the world. The world tells us we will never be thin enough, beautiful enough, or sexy enough. The world tells us we can never get past the choices we've made or the abuse others have forced on our bodies. The world tells us if we just do a little bit more or look a little different, then we will be accepted—but we never are.

God has a different message. God tells us it is impossible for Him to love us more. Nothing we do, have done, or will do can ever change that. He already accepts us—we can stop striving.

Believing this truth frees us from the cycle of giving our bodies too much or too little attention. We realize that no matter how we try to change, manipulate, or ignore our bodies, we will not find satisfaction until we receive God's unconditional love for us. And it's that love that motivates us to love what God made.

So when we try to be perfect by the world's standards, we fail. When we receive the truth that we are fearfully and wonderfully made, we want to care for God's remarkable creation well.

Coming Home

Artists throughout the ages have tried to make Jesus look good—perhaps better than He actually looked. After all, we don't want to think of God as residing in a normal-looking, average-built body. I've never seen an image of an overweight Jesus hanging on the cross.

I've never seen an image of Jesus with no hair. We imagine Him to be extraordinary. Handsome. Eye-catching, yet of course humble about it. But what if Jesus was ordinary? Average? Physically unappealing?

In what are called the Suffering Servant prophecies in Isaiah (52:13—53:12), we read that Jesus "had no beauty or majesty to attract us to him, nothing in his appearance that we should desire him" (53:2). Yet Jesus was the perfect human. And a satisfied soul.

Physical prowess, strength, and beauty reside only in the skin and bone structure of our souls' address. We're told that beauty fades (Prov. 31:30), but the soul never will fade. Read what Jesus said and consider his implications for your body.

> *The Spirit of the Lord is on me,*
> *because he has anointed me*
> *to preach good news to the poor.*
> *He has sent me to proclaim freedom for the prisoners*
> *and recovery of sight for the blind,*
> *to release the oppressed,*
> *to proclaim the year of the Lord's favor. (Luke*
> *4:18–19)*

How we need this good news for our bodies—bodies that feel imprisoned in our genetic makeup, past choices, or abuse. Jesus reminds us that anyone who is imprisoned in their bodies can experience freedom and recovery and live in the Lord's favor.

It is true that one day we will have new bodies. This is the soulful promise given us concerning heaven. One day, disability, DNA, memories, and fears will not hurt us any more. No soul will suffer with Alzheimer's or crippling arthritis. In eternity we will live in perfection without blemish, pain, or limp.

But treating our bodies with honor and respect on this earth is an act of worship and an act of faith. It is an acknowledgment that even our bodily weaknesses and needs can draw us to God.

In her book on body image and eating disorders, author Sharon Hersh points out that in the story of the prodigal son, it was the son's appetite that both drove him from home and brought him back. His hunger for living independently took him away from his loving father, but his physical hunger caused him to return home: "He was so hungry he would have eaten the corncobs in the pig slop, but no one would give him any" (Luke 15:16 MSG).

As Hersh writes,

> God understands hunger. He knows the places
> our hunger can take us—sometimes to places of
> indulgence, shame, or deprivation. And just as the
> father in the story hopes for his son's return while he
> daily watches and waits for him, God hopes that our
> hunger will eventually lead us home…. [Hunger] for
> physical food, to fit in and be liked, to look good …
> can lead us home.[9]

Perfect Connection

The weakness of the church of my youth was not the enjoyment of food. Our good God created us to experience both physical and spiritual pleasures. My church's weakness was the enjoyment of a bodily pleasure, or need, without understanding its connection to the soul.

By choosing to make the body-soul connection today, we can live as whole souls knowing that how we treat our bodies is really how we are treating our souls.

In his book *The Gift of Pain,* Dr. Paul Brand writes of the physical joys God designed us to have every day.

> *All activities important for the body's survival and health provide physical pleasure when we do them right. The sex act, which ensures the survival of the species, gives pleasure. Eating food is not a chore but a pleasure. Even the body's maintenance task of excretion brings pleasure.... Hard work and exercise, which may seem like pain in the short term, paradoxically lead to pleasure in the longer term.*

Brand goes on to describe a time in his life when he worked a construction job involving hard physical labor. He enjoyed his fit body and the weekend walks he was able to take without having to stop to catch his breath.

> *On these walks ... I would suddenly become aware of the immense pleasure of a body working according to design. The Hebrew language has a wonderful word,* shalom, *which expresses an overall sense of peace and*

well-being, a positive state of wholeness and health. I
felt shalom, *as if all my body's cells were calling out*
in unison, "All is well."[10]

Brand is not describing how great he felt about how he looked, the number of pounds he could bench press, or pleasure in seeing others admire him. He had a greater joy: a sense that his body, mind, and spirit were at peace with one another. We can choose to be optimistic about how we view our bodies and our health. It's a proven fact that optimism breeds health, whereas unmanaged anger can double the risk of not only physical heart disease but an impaired spiritual heart as well.

This is what Jesus is helping me work toward as I continue this journey of soul care and body care. By caring for my body, I am honoring my soul—honoring God within me, honoring Jesus within me. That's a spiritual reality that motivates me to do more than lose weight or get more sleep! It reminds me to appreciate the communication, the beauty, the perfect design of our body-soul connection. It reminds me that one day, all will be well. *Shalom.*

■ ■ ■ ■ ■

Questions for Reflection

1. Read 1 Corinthians 3:16–17 from several different translations. Do the same thing with Psalm 139. How do these verses speak to the connection between our souls and our bodies?

2. Create a chart highlighting wellness in your body and soul. (In the appendix see "Charting the Body/Soul Connection" on page 220.) A notebook or journal will suffice for this. On the X axis draw a timeline throughout your day. The Y axis will represent your moods, your emotions, and energy levels through the day. Split the Y axis with a line creating a positive area above the line and a negative areas below the line. Next consider the times in your day when you felt physically well and when you felt physically poor. Write about your soul with a different colored pen. Note the well times and poor times, the times you felt disappointed, lonely, afraid, and angry and how this might affect your body as well as your soul. Try this for a month and see what you learn about your body-soul connection.

3. Create a story version of the timeline of your life so far and put marks on the timeline when you had major or minor realizations about your health, lifestyle issues, and illnesses that significantly impacted you. When did you become more aware and more health conscious? What was going on around and in you?

4. What do you feel is the role of the body-soul connection in Christian life today? Does your

church or faith community have an emphasis on
this? Why or why not? How can you envision the
body-soul connection being shared in the life of
your church and community?

5. Find a highly recommended book about the body-
   soul connection. Read some reviews on Amazon
   or Google before you purchase a book and learn
   all you can on this fascinating subject.

Notes

1 Chris Crowley and Henry S. Lodge, *Younger Next Year* (New York: Workman Publishing Company, 2007), 324.
2 Michael Strassfeld, "The Spirituality of Food," http://www.myjewishlearning.com/practices/Ethics/Our_Bodies/Health_and_Healing/Caring_for_Ones_Health/Spirituality_of_Food.shtml (accessed July 24, 2009).
3 Dallas Willard, "The Human Body and Spiritual Growth," *Christian Educator's Handbook*, http://www.dwillard.org/articles/artview.asp?artID=34.
4 Barbara Brown Taylor, *An Altar in the World* (New York: HarperOne, 2009), 38.
5 For more information on Fasting, consider reading Lynn Babb's *Fasting* (IVP, 2009).
6 As quoted in Stephen W. Smith, *Embracing Soul Care* (Grand Rapids, MI: Kregel, 2006), 128.
7 YMCA, "History of the YMCA Movement," http://www.ymca.net/about_the_ymca/history_of_the_ymca.html.
8 Henri Nouwen, *Life of the Beloved: Spiritual Living in a Secular World* (New York: Crossroads Publishing Company, 2002), 33.
9 Sharon A. Hersh, *Mom, I Feel Fat!* (Colorado Springs, CO: WaterBrook Press, 2001), 205–206.
10 Paul Brand and Philip Yancey, *The Gift of Pain* (Grand Rapids, MI: Zondervan, 1997), 297–298.

10

Soul Companions

Choosing Your Friends

A mirror reflects a man's face, but what he is really
like is shown by the kind of friends he chooses.
— *Proverbs 27:19 TLB*

My friends are my estate.
— *Emily Dickinson*

The word *companion* offers us a beautiful and stirring picture of friendship. *Companion,* in its original French context, means "with bread." The word paints a picture of two hungry beggars looking for the same thing: bread.

Isn't that what we do in friendship? We are so hungry to be filled with love, so thirsty to have our souls' reservoirs filled with acceptance and affirmation. We hunt till we find it, crave it until we are satisfied by it, and pray like crazy that God will provide it. Without this kind of true companionship, we are left to search alone, hunt by ourselves, beggars, hopefully not giving up in despair.

Social networking is exploding in the first decade of the twenty-first century as a means for people to find one another. But you know that, right? You're getting in touch with old school friends you haven't seen in years, becoming "friends" once more. We update the status of our lives, from the ridiculous to the sublime, and carry a sense of being connected. But I do wonder sometimes how much our souls are fed with just status updates. The truth is cyber bread is different from the bread Jesus offers.

From Adam's earliest days, we learn that it is "not good for the man to be alone" (Gen. 2:18). Yet many of us live in the land of "not good," having failed to find a soul companion with whom we can eat our bread and drink our lattes, face-to-face. The "not good" state of our souls is something that we must give attention to. If the soul is to be cared for, we must realize that this care happens alongside others.

Ruth's words to Naomi are a powerful expression of a type of relationship that today almost seems mythical. "Where you go, I go; and where you live, I'll live. Your people are my people, your God is my god; where you die, I'll die, and that's where I'll be buried, so help me GOD—not even death itself is going to come between us!" (Ruth 1:16–17 MSG).

For many of us, nothing stirs the soul quite like sharing the journey of life with a person whom you love and from whom you receive love. Listen to David's words following the death of his soul-friend, Jonathan.

> *O my dear brother Jonathan,*
> *I'm crushed by your death.*
> *Your friendship was a miracle-wonder,*
> *love far exceeding anything I've known—*
> *or ever hope to know. (2 Sam. 1:26 MSG)*

When friendship works miracles to assuage our loneliness, when another soul offers us love that quenches the thirst within, when companionship gives what nothing else in life can ever hope to give, then we are truly cared for deep in our souls.

Lonely World

The idea of community is often romanticized, filled with illusions and exaggerated promises about what community can actually deliver. Add to that the frustration over the work involved in building it and then the emotions that vary wildly from the excitement of finally having a BFF (best friend forever) to the agony over a once-promising relationship gone sour. So, as much as the concept of community is promoted through our churches, support groups, and social-networking sites, we can still come up empty when it comes to actually experiencing another soul. We'd like to have the kind of friendship we read about in the Bible between David and Jonathan or between Ruth and Naomi. But we're not there.

It's interesting how our vocabulary today is shifting in the way it refers to community. Companies have changed their "personnel departments" to "human resources." (The more sterile term is perhaps more fitting when people are reduced to "resources" and not affirmed as living souls.) The term *networking* was formerly used for machines and computers, but now we use it for how we interact as human beings. We say, "Let's catch up sometime," meaning share the chronological calendar of our lives with our "doing" rather than sharing our souls. And those on Facebook, all 320 million of us, can now "friend" and "unfriend" people with a click of the mouse.

Unfortunately, the church is rather weak in this area. Because of the emphasis on worship and teaching in the last thirty years, most church buildings have majored on worship space at the expense of places to meet, gather, and sit down with one another and actually talk. That kind of dynamic might be more likely to happen today in a Starbucks or some quiet venue with conducive lighting, soft music, and intimately arranged tables.

Today many of us are giving up on the church and are fleeing to have our new "church" in coffeehouses or someplace else that's wired so we can be connected to a Facebook "friend." We're doing this though without our souls ever touching, without ever really looking into the eyes of another soul to see and be seen, to know and be known, to discover and be discovered. Ruth and Naomi did more than just "touch base." When David and Jonathan met together, it appears they did more than chat.

Yet the evidence suggests that few of us are experiencing this type of soulful relationship. In a *Washington Post* article from June 2006, we read, "Americans are far more socially isolated today than they were two decades ago, and a sharply growing number of people say they have no one in whom they can confide.… A quarter of Americans say they have no one with whom they can discuss personal troubles, more than double the number who were similarly isolated in 1985."[1]

We're told that the majority of business partnerships fail these days. Only one in two marriages will survive beyond twenty years. And team conflict, or the inability to get along, is the number-one reason for missionaries to be sent "home." But we tell ourselves that friendship along the lines of David and Jonathan is indeed rare. So we settle for just getting by, and our souls are deprived of richness, satisfaction, and joy because we put effort into something false, a substitute that gives only the appearance of being connected with one another.

The soul was not made for pseudo-friendships. When we settle for them, we are choosing to settle for far less than we were made for.

True friendship and the building of authentic community was so vital to the writers of the New Testament that they used the expression "one another" more than fifty times. We are told to love one another, accept one another, serve one another, pray for one another, build one another up, and confess to one another. These terms might seem more foreign to us than natural. Living with so much aloneness can make us skeptical of the possibilities of a soul connection with anyone.

Dance of the Porcupines

To craft a soulful friendship, we must first be honest with ourselves about what we can offer another person in a relationship. The truth is if I'm wounded (and I am), I will offer my wounds, my fears of being rejected, my entire history and unhealthy patterns of relating and still hope that I can connect with another living soul.

This is like asking one porcupine to dance with another porcupine. We can get stuck, pierced, and wounded by the quills we all wear when getting close to one another. My fear of your quills hurting me may make me pull back or not give myself to you so fully. I might even stay at the edge.

If I was badly hurt by a previous friendship, I can bring the infection of bitterness, resentment, and hurt to you. My own disease of soul might infect everyone with malaise.

We mistakenly assume that one broken person plus another broken person equals a whole. We may feel complete when we find our "soul mate." But our math is wrong. One broken person plus another broken person just equals more broken people. What we hoped for in another person could quickly become dysfunctional, codependent, and sick! The best we can do on our own is to compound the brokenness in the room. We lean heavily into one another, expecting—sometimes demanding—that he or she give us what we need. We can cry together in each other's beer, but that doesn't add up to a soul friendship. Songwriter David Wilcox expresses the insight this way.

> *You cannot make me happy.*
> *Not when I'm empty inside of me....*
> *My misery'd love to have your company....*
> *We cannot trade empty for empty.*[2]

Together with Christ

Friendship at the soul level is that place Aelred of Rievaulx described in the twelfth century: "Here we are, you and I, and I hope a third, Christ is in our midst." A soul friendship is that sacred gift through which one is understood and known, where no defense is needed, where love is cherished and it feels like "shelter to speak to you."[3] A soul friendship is an open place for another soul to emerge, a safe place for the action of friendship making, which is no easy task.

When Jesus said, "Where two or three come together in my name, there am I with them" (Matt. 18:20), He pledged His presence. This sacred presence is what transforms ordinary friendship into soulful friends. We experience God in our midst: Emmanuel. We say like the disciples said on the road to Emmaus when Jesus walked with them: "Were not our hearts burning within us while he [Jesus] talked with us?" (Luke 24:32). Soul friendship is the experience of the burning heart phenomenon. It is where the heart begins to burn like the bush began to burn in front of Moses—the place where God is encountered and experienced.

When this happened to Moses, he "turned aside" to look at the bush more closely (see Ex. 3:3 KJV). When our hearts begin to burn within us, we, too, can turn aside to our friend and witness that there is another in our midst. We are not alone. We are tasting the presence of God, which is our true and necessary bread.

A lunch becomes more than a lunch when this happens with a friend. We feast on food that is more than fish and chips. We offer to each other the bread of companionship that is filling, satisfying, and life-giving. We do much more than "catch up." It is communion. We are enjoying Jesus in our midst. Soul friends want this sacred presence.

Present with You and Moving toward "Us"

When our understanding of soul friendship is raised beyond "checking in" and "catching up" with one another, we move to become aware of the presence of the other, who is God with us. We offer ourselves to one another and feast in the fellowship that can transform us. We are present to each other and we are in the presence of God. Let me explain.

When we are present to each other, we move away from the illusion that everything revolves around us. Friendship is a movement from *me* to *we*. Christian psychologist and author David Benner writes, "To be present to you means that I must be prepared, temporarily, to be absent from me."[4] My selfish desires to be heard and understood must be put aside for the sake of the other. It's not about just me. It's about us.

We consciously move from the journey alone to the journey together. When we "love one another deeply, from the heart" (1 Pet. 1:22), we move out of our own hearts into the sacred space of our friends—where peace and fear coexist, where trust and doubt find an equal dwelling place, where secrets are so embedded and darkness so great that we long for someone to come bring us light. The poet Mary Oliver says it well: "The heart has many dungeons. Bring the light. Bring the light."

It is in sacred friendship, and perhaps only there, that we can learn to move from myself to ourselves. In a soul friendship, we move out of our dungeons and into the light of not only each other's presence but also the very presence of Christ—the true light. Benner helps us again: "When I live with 'me' as the basic reference point for life, I experience a fundamental existential alienation. Not only am I alienated from others, but paradoxically I am also alienated from my deepest self. For my deepest and truest self is not an isolated self but finds its meaning and fulfillment only in the 'we' or community."[5] In a soul friendship, we die to our false self and learn the joy and sheer grace of finally being accepted as we truly are. Here is unparalleled safety and grace that no other entity in life offers us but soul friends.

Sharing All the Heart with All Your Soul

Do you have hidden chambers of your heart that no one else has access to? I'm sure you do; I know I do. Medical doctors tell us that the human heart has four chambers. I would like to use these chambers to illustrate our friendships.

Chamber One is the surface level of connecting to another person. Here we share basic information about each other: "What do you do for a living? Where do you live? Where did you grow up?" These are beginner conversations.

Chamber Two conversations go a bit deeper. Here we share affinity and common interests: "I'm from North Carolina, too! Which city? Where did you go to high school? I love pizza, too!" A basic affinity begins to surface in Chamber Two in which we begin to like and wonder if this new acquaintance could grow into something more. *I wonder if we could be good friends?* we say to ourselves.

Chamber Three is where we share some of our story—the good along with the bad. We may talk about our job situations, being on the brink of financial collapse, maybe even revealing some of the skeletons in our pasts. We try to be reciprocal in what we give to each other and also receive. Rarely, however, does friendship move past Chamber Three.

But what the Bible is very clear on is that way down deep in each one of us is that place I am calling the Fourth Chamber—that place that holds secrets that no one knows; that dark place where little light has been cast, where hurts, wounds, and hemorrhaging places of our souls dwell.

Soul friendship is the journey of sharing all the chambers of the heart with all the chambers of another's heart and discovering the pulse of God in the midst of all of it. It is precisely this Fourth Chamber that Jesus described when He said,

> *Listen now, all of you—take this to heart. It's not*
> *what you swallow that pollutes your life; it's what you*
> *vomit—that's the real pollution…. Don't you see that*
> *what you swallow can't contaminate you? … It's what*
> *comes out of a person that pollutes: obscenities, lusts,*
> *thefts, murders, adulteries, greed, depravity, deceptive*
> *dealings, carousing, mean looks, slander, arrogance,*
> *foolishness—all these are vomit from the heart. There*
> *is the source of your pollution. (Mark 7:14–23 MSG)*

The Fourth Chamber is the domain that good friends, tested friends, and proven friends can explore together. It is the chamber that yields the highest rewards of personal transformation and it is the most challenging chamber to enter with one another.

Friendship becomes sacred when we allow the Fourth Chamber pollution to become clean so that with one heart and one mouth we can live free and be free. We cannot do this alone. Fourth Chamber conversations require trust, safety, and an invitation to "go there" with a friend, though "there" may be scary and unexplored. Yet you trust your friend that he will not hurt you or pull a knife on you when you stumble into pollution.

As I've mentioned before, the "one another" passages in the New Testament are mentioned more than the Great Commission—more than tithing, more than praying, and more than confessing your sins. They are evidently in our Bible to show us how to live in healthy relationships that are reciprocal and life-giving. Have you ever been in a conversation with a "friend" in which that friend dominated the conversation, perhaps the entire time you were together? It's alarming when you walk away from such a time and realize that there was no space—no invitation for you to share your own thoughts, feelings, and experiences. The movements away from yourself in conversation are the necessary steps to close the gap with another person. Soulful friendship is reciprocal. It is give and take and not either one all the time.

When we are driven by our fears that we might not be listened to well, we can become so anxious to be heard that we demand it from each other. But true love in friendship "does not demand its own way" (1 Cor. 13:5 NLT). It requires a certain risk to do this because privately we hope for our friends to turn to us and say, "Tell me about what's going on with you."

Helping Each Other Get Started

Despite the fact that I know many of the often-quoted "one another" passages in the Bible, despite the fact that I know I cannot take off the grave clothes of Lazarus without a friend to help free me, despite the fact that I know I should love everyone and be at peace with all people, I still find myself a novice when it comes to building a deep soul friendship with anyone other than my wife and a very few others. There are no seminars, conferences, or retreats on how to be a good friend. But shouldn't there be? We don't naturally know how to do this, do we?

God knows I have tried and tried. I flip-flop between giving up and somehow mustering up the courage to try again. Soul friendship is hard. It demands my all, and sometimes I'm just not willing to give that much. I want something left over for me. And then I look around and I have no one with which to beg bread today. In my heart, I am alone. Again.

We have so many roles in life that we are often clueless to know how to begin. When my sons married their wives, I did not know how to be a good father-in-law. So I told my first daughter-in-law, Sara, "I'm new at this. You need to help me. Coach me. I want to learn and be a really good dad for you." Couldn't we do the same thing with a friend?

What would it take for us to be more honest and say things like, "I don't know how to go the long haul with you"? What if we were honest with how our transient work lives (which require some of us to be like corporate migrants, moving every season to a new place to start a new life) have impacted our friendships? What if we poured a new foundation for a relationship by saying things like, "I've never gone the distance with anyone. I'm new. I'm broken, but I'm willing to learn"?

Peter Scazerro, pastor and writer, has told us that it is impossible to be spiritually mature while remaining emotionally immature.[6] Our emotional immaturity most often manifests itself in our attempts to make friends. We bring our dirty laundry with us into every group we try to join and every friendship we seek to build. We need to recognize that spiritual growth is growth in every area and aspect of our lives, including friendship and community.

The Few Jesus Trusted

The gospel of Mark tells us that Jesus selected a few as close friends. "Jesus went up on a mountainside and called to him *those he wanted,* and they came to him (Mark 3:14). Jesus wanted a close circle of friends. He called certain individuals, not everyone, into this inner circle. His choice was not random nor by chance. He singled out individuals to step inside the circumference of his own soul to gain there the truth that would change their lives forever.

Jesus chose twelve men to be "with Him." His with time included lots of walking, taking the time to lie down in the shade and tell stories, maybe even some jokes; time to be with one another by going into town and buying food at the market that would become more than a meal. It was time that was shared, time when they lingered together, time that became the bridge for souls to cross over into one another's personal space and see what was really going on. In these intimate settings, we see Jesus making time to let His companions ask for more clarification and also taking the time to confront them when they had eyes but couldn't see.

Yet it is interesting that Jesus did not offer to share His soul in this way with any and everyone. He chose only a few; therein lies a huge clue for us. Friendship, if it is to be true and real, can probably flower only in the hearts of a few. You may have 428 people who know you on Facebook, but I don't believe you have 428 true friends. Jesus distinguished between what He would give the crowds and what He would offer the few. He taught the public, but He offered his most private teaching, His most intimate secrets to the few—to the ones whom He thought could handle it and handle Him.

The stuff of the soul is too complex, too valuable, too multilayered to be given out like a buffet where people come and take what they want and leave the rest for someone else. The soul sometimes has unwanted things to offer, like any buffet often does. Who likes green peas when they've been sitting out a long time and are shriveled and wrinkled? My soul has wrinkled and dried-out parts, I'm sure, and I often feel like no one wants those pieces of myself. There are places in me so mixed up that it looks like succotash where the orangish and yellow niblets and unrecognizable chopped-up pieces seem unappetizing. I find some of my acquaintances head straight to the sweetness of my soul but do not want the sour. They want the meat, but without the blood. They want the savory, but not the bland.

Listen to Emerson speak of true soul friendship: "I do not wish to treat friendships daintily, but with roughest courage. When they are real, they are not glass threads or frostwork, but the solidest thing we know."[7]

Love, the Foundation

David Benner reminds us that "love is the acid test of Christian spirituality." Either we are growing to be more loving or we are not growing at all in our souls. Benner goes on, "If we are not becoming more loving, something is seriously wrong."[8] Soul friendships are the place where love is fostered, nurtured, and given. It is also the primary place where love is received. It is the place where the soul connects in love, to love and to be loved. Jesus knew well that the love He came to teach about—the love He died for—was radical and very, very costly.

Love for one another is the proof that we love God. It's not the amount we know in our heads but the love we extend in our hearts that gives witness to a world gone mad that there is another way in which to live. Jesus' friend John tell us, "My beloved friends, let us continue to love each other since love comes from God. Everyone who loves is born of God and experiences a relationship with God. The person who refuses to love doesn't know the first thing about God, because God is love—so you can't know him if you don't love" (1 John 4:7-8 MSG).

We simply cannot assume that we know how to give this kind of love, though our souls yearn for it. Paul was elemental in his teaching to the Christians at Corinth about how to really love when you don't feel you have anything to give. He breaks down the huge word *love* into bite-size chunks that we need to pause and digest. Assuming that we actually know how to love one another is like my assuming that I know how to be a good husband to my wife. I've been married for thirty years, but I'm still learning about love and about being a true companion to my wife.

Read Paul's words here, and no matter what season of life you find yourself in right now, see if they don't challenge you to stretch and grow into this love.

> *Love never gives up.*
> *Love cares more for others than for self.*
> *Love doesn't want what it doesn't have.*
> *Love doesn't strut,*
> *Doesn't have a swelled head,*
> *Doesn't force itself on others,*
> *Isn't always "me first,"*
> *Doesn't fly off the handle,*
> *Doesn't keep score of the sins of others,*
> *Doesn't revel when others grovel,*
> *Takes pleasure in the flowering of truth,*

Puts up with anything,
Trusts God always,
Always looks for the best,
Never looks back,
But keeps going to the end. (1 Cor.13:4–7 MSG)

Anam Cara

Just before our son deployed to Iraq, a few friends gathered one evening, and we put Jordan in the middle. We laid our hands on him
and his new wife, Sara, and we spoke words—words that were filled
with emotion, hope, and fear all mixed together. When we said the
last *amen*, we all hugged. It helped. To try and describe that evening
with words might lessen the sacredness of that time. All I can say
is *it simply helped.* These precious people are *anam cara* to us. John
O'Donohue explains,

> *The Celtic understanding of friendship finds its*
> *inspiration and culmination in the sublime notion*
> *of the* anam cara. Anam *is the Gaelic word for*
> *soul;* cara *is the word for friend. So* anam cara
> *means soul friend. The anam cara was a person to*
> *whom you could reveal the hidden intimacies of*
> *your life. This friendship was an act of recognition*
> *and belonging. When you had an anam cara, your*
> *friendship cut across all convention and category.*
> *You were joined in an ancient and eternal way with*

the friend of your soul....With the anam cara you
could share your innermost self, your mind and your
heart. This friendship was an act of recognition and
belonging.... In everyone's life there is a great need
for an anam cara, a soul friend. In this love, you are
understood as you are without mask or pretension.
The superficial and functional lies and half-truths of
acquaintance fall away, you can be as you really are.[9]

"You are like nobody since I love you."
–Pablo Neruda

■ ■ ■ ■ ■

Questions for Reflection

1. Read Ecclesiastes 4:9–12. Why is friendship better? What kind of friendship is described in this passage?

2. How would you describe the level of friendships in your spiritual journey?

3. What have been the greatest obstacles for you to experiencing friendship the way the author describes?

4. What is your reaction to the author's description
   of the "four chambers of the heart"? How does
   this play out in a few of the relationships you have
   at the present time?

5. Do you have an *anam cara*? If not, what are a
   few ways you could be an *anam cara* to someone
   else?

Notes

1 Shankar Vedantam, "Social Isolation Growing in U.S., Study Says," *Washington Post*, June
   23, 2006.
2 David Wilcox, *Break in the Cup*, Midnight Ocean Bonfire Music, © 1994, Irving Music Inc.
3 Emily Dickinson, "Emily Dickinson: Early Feminist Essays" (pub. 1886–1915),
   http://www.earlywomenmasters.net/essays/authors/higginson/twh_dickinson11.html
   (accessed August 4, 2009).
4 David Benner, *Sacred Companions: The Gift of Spiritual Friendship & Direction* (Downers
   Grove, IL: InterVarsity Press), 50.
5 Ibid., 93.
6 I highly recommend Peter Scazzero's book *Emotionally Healthy Spirituality: Unleash the
   Power of Life in Christ* (Franklin, TN: Integrity Publishers, 2006).
7 Ralph Waldo Emerson, Essays (London: Robson, Levey, and Franklyn, 1848), 184.
8 David Benner, *Surrender to Love: Discovering the Heart of Christian Spirituality* (Downers
   Grove, IL: InterVarsity Press, 2003), 90.
9 John O'Donohue, *Anam Cara: A Book of Celtic Wisdom* (New York: Harper Perennial,
   1997), 13–14.

11

Soul Action

Moving from Choice to Action

Therefore, my dear ones, as you have always
obeyed [my suggestions], so now, not only
[with the enthusiasm you would show] in
my presence but much more because I am
absent, work out (cultivate, carry out to the
goal, and fully complete) your own salvation
with reverence and awe and trembling (self-
distrust, with serious caution, tenderness of
conscience, watchfulness against temptation,
timidly shrinking from whatever might offend
God and discredit the name of Christ).
—*Philippians 2:12 AB*

I shall now try to look calmly at
myself and begin to act inwardly.
—*Søren Kierkegaard*

It's not enough to have read this book and think we've "got it." No,
taking custody of one's soul does not work that way. There must be

action. Action steps are our ways to "work out" our own salvation
(Phil. 2:12). Without any action, we will remain in our shame that
says, "I know I should do better. I know I should live differently."
We are frightened of giving up our illusions of ourselves. As long as
we deny and dismiss aspects of our nature that need change, we will
never grow up—no matter what our chronological ages. Taking care
of our business is practicing spiritual responsibility.

If you have found that the choices described in *Soul Custody*
speak to your heart, then bring this home to where you live. It's time
to work through the implications and practice day-by-day soul care.

Here, let's try to converge all I have been saying and consider
some practical and down-to-earth advice on how to gain back our
souls and maintain a custody so wonderful that we will always want
to give care to our souls.

Admitting the Truth

You might think that the message of caring for your soul would meet
little to no resistance. Nothing could be further from the truth. As
I share this message with individuals and groups, I always find an
undercurrent of strong resistance. When that resistance is tapped, it
threatens to blow off steam like Old Faithful. Old messages from our
family of origins or culture echo loudly within us: "The world is a big
place. Stick with a safe path. Don't take risks. You'll fail."

Some feel threatened because such talk of the soul sounds more
New Age than biblical. But as you have seen, every single aspect that
we have explored in this book is anchored in the Judeo-Christian
Bible. In a sense, there's very little new here. What *is* new is the

diagnosis of our hearts' and souls' annihilation, our feelings of not being able to cope, and the violence we are living with while ignoring the essence of our God-given life. Caring for our souls is ageless, and there is a need in every season, every culture, and every single soul to heed this message.

We have so long been gripped by the notion of burning out for God that our lives produce the toxic fumes of drivenness. We take Jesus' offer of rest and turn it into an invitation to run an unending marathon. We must bow in recognition of the simple fact that we have lived our lives according to the beat of a drum that says, "March! March! March! More! More! More! Do! Do! Do!" It is the message of the Egyptian slave drivers who whipped the backs and slapped the brows of the children of Israel, people not created to live in such dire conditions. We were not either.

When we admit this, we will soon realize that the very platform of the life we have been building—the life that we thought we would enjoy—will start creaking from the weight and bowing from the pressure. We simply have to admit that life is more than adding more, doing more, and working more to our already bowed backs.

We may have to admit that we have not really understood the gospel at all and have allowed our souls to be hijacked by people and messages that have copied the world's standards and human ways of measuring progress at the expense of our souls. Admitting the truth about how we have gotten into this state means taking a long look at our souls. It may require more honesty and responsibility than we have ever been capable of, but that's where it begins. Self-examination is hard—it's for those who are ready to live their lives as responsible adults.

Facing the truth about how you are doing is facing the truth about your soul. Don't deny that you need to do this. Don't ignore the warning signals that your soul gives you, such as stress, depression, lack of joy, relational strife, spiritual dryness, anxiety levels, preoccupation with daydreams and fantasies, time spent using technology, and more.

Neither should you ignore the positive aspects of your own fulfillment, including inner peace, contentment with life, spiritual aliveness, and exuberance about life. Instead, let these indicators, positive or negative, help you and others discern what state your soul really is in.

Admitting that we are "in trouble" or experiencing any symptoms in the above paragraph helps to bring us to our knees. That is a great starting place. Kneel before God and tell Him about the parts of your life—which silos—are just out of control. Believe that God can help you. Turn your will over to God and begin to take responsibility for a life that will be more expansive, more soulful, and much more reflective. Your soul will do much more than survive; you'll thrive.

Giving Yourself Permission

No one gives me permission to follow Jesus and love God more than I do. I have to learn to give myself permission to do what is right. If I keep waiting for someone else to validate my own desire to do what is right for me and what will honor God, I may be waiting a long time. I may grow older without ever hearing someone who will become a champion for my soul. I may not have a better soul advocate than myself. I have to believe this.

If you're like me, you may have to give up the myth that "out there" somewhere is a perfect and ideal friend whom you may meet one day and who is really going to be "for" you. The person you might be waiting on is really yourself. Friends may encourage you, preachers may inspire you, and a spouse may help you, but in the end no one can care for your soul like you can. Embracing that fact is learning to be good to yourself and to honor the God who made you to be the real you! It is easier to enter the flow of life without having to hide out because you are ashamed of choices you have made.

Choosing to Be Yourself

Because we are individually made and not formed out of the same mold, to care for our souls, we must also choose to be our true selves. That big choice has many implications that you need to think through. Being true to your own soul means learning the ways that will work for you. Some choices you implement that fit you and work for you may be different and more complex or simple than your friend or spouse chooses to care for his or her own soul. What works for me may not work for you.

For too long we have wrongly assumed that all people learn in the same way. Thankfully now there is more evidence that informs us correctly that some of us will learn in far different ways how to care for our souls and grow in our faith.

Some of the categories of our souls and the ways we learn include these:

- Some of us are *verbal learners*. We like words and the meanings of them. We like books and read and enjoy

them. If this style of learning fits you, read some of
the recommended books that I have mentioned
here as well as ones you are aware of. Also, consider
starting a small group in which members can read
and discuss what they are learning.

- Some of us are *logical learners*. We enjoy numbers,
  sequence, and problem solving. We have strong
  reasoning skills and like order to how we are taught.
  If this describes you, you may want to do a survey
  of the history of all the ways men and women have
  tried to care for their souls. Two excellent resources
  for this are Gerald Sittser's *Water from a Deep Well*
  and John McNeil's *The History of the Cure of the
  Souls*.

- Some of us are *visual learners*. We are creative, enjoy
  the arts of all kinds, and find ourselves stimulated
  by imagination and curiosity. I love the term *visio
  divina*, which is honoring how we view art, nature,
  and more through our eyes and take this into our
  souls. Once, when as a family we were viewing a Van
  Gogh exhibit, our guide was so informative and so
  interesting that one of our boys said, "Dad, this was
  the best part of our trip. I feel like Van Gogh is a part
  of us now."

- Some of us are *auditory learners*. We love language
  and music that stirs our souls and makes us feel things
  that no book or message ever could. Movement and
  rhythm captivate us. If this fits you, you may enjoy

listening to an audio book. Music may move you and bring you back to life.

- Some of us are *physical learners*. We are athletic and active. We enjoy exercise and movement and are fascinated by the body. One team of men came to our retreat recently to work on our project: making a larger retreat facility out of a big red barn. I led the men in an overview of how builders and carpenters were honored by God and were the first to be filled with the Spirit. It validated the men and workers and gave them a sense of pride in their hard physical labor while on a mission trip.

- Some of us are *extroverted learners*. We thrive when we are with people. We like teams and working together. You might find it interesting to do some character studies of major biblical characters and see if you can determine their personality profile and how they might have cared or not cared for their souls. As you consider the life of Jesus, trace how you see his own methods and ways of caring for his soul. Consider using the gospel of Luke, who was a medical doctor and used the lens of his own training to embed interesting insights into the lifestyle of Jesus.

- Some of us are *introverted learners*. We find solitude necessary and we withdraw often to be alone and are okay with it. We work independently and are self-motivated. Consider doing a survey of the great truths monastic communities and spiritual writers who lived alone offer us. Read Thomas Merton's *The Wisdom of the Desert* as a valuable guide into the hearts and souls of the desert fathers and mothers who left the cities and lived out their lives in solitude.

• The important thing is to keep learning, keep growing, and keep caring for your own soul.

If we are interested in how we are spiritually formed and develop in life, we need to understand the uniqueness of our souls and cease our efforts to only learn about life, God, and our own souls' needs in one fashion. There are multiple ways to experience God and guard our hearts. As you think this through, for the sake of your own soul, give yourself permission to explore what way is really life-giving for you. Then stay with that way and watch yourself to see if you are feeling cared for.

Integrating Your Life

Remember the silos built on farms that independently hold different grains? One silo sticks up here. Another sticks up over there. And they are completely separate from each other.

Many of us have used that same method of having categories to make life work for us. One silo for my job, one for my family, one for my body, one for my church, one for my spouse, and one for God. What you have seen in this book, by contrast, is that there are no silos for the soul. None. Everything is connected.

I'm going to describe a homemade device that is capable of

showing you the deep connections within your soul. It may help if you'd actually make what I'm going to describe.[1]

Take a piece of wood about one foot square. Hammer rows of nails around the edges of the piece of wood (at least three nails on each row). Then attach rubber bands from one nail to every other nail. As you are doing this, imagine that one rubber band is your family; another, your work; another, your spouse; another, your body; another, your money; another, your relationship with God; and so on.

Now pull one of the rubber bands and quickly let it go. When one band is pulled, stretched, and stressed, every other band feels the tension. Every single rubber band vibrates when only one band is stretched and pulled.

This is an easy way to see how caring for the soul works. When you feel stressed-out because of your work, then your spouse and family are impacted. Your money situation might also be affected, because it might feel as if it is going to snap or break due to the tension. That stress affects everyone around you—even your dog. Trust me—my golden retriever knows!

Becoming Curious

Our resistance to do anything about our spiritual conditions is interesting. After reading this book, you may feel inspired. Or you may feel the need for a long nap by the fire. Becoming curious about what stirs inside you when you consider this topic can be very revealing to you. Your curiosity about your soul will make you more self-aware, more God-aware, and more spiritually sensitive than if you were merely living your life on autopilot.

Curiosity is a good word to help us learn how to care for the soul. Remember, the soul is shy and needs to feel safe to emerge with God, other people, and even ourselves.

Be careful what you take into your soul. Pay attention to what you allow your soul to partake in. Rather than "taking it all in," or feeling like you have to "drink from a fire hydrant," learn to say *enough*. No soul can drink from a fire hydrant, so why do we try to teach in a way that mimics such absurd behavior? People can become obsessed with learning—even in the spiritual life. By attending this meeting, those conferences, and that event, we allow our souls to be overfed and undernourished.

My dog, Laz, a golden retriever, is so fixated on food that once we pour his food into his bowl, you had better step back, because he attacks his bowl with gusto. Some Christians are the same. They want "meat" all the time—and red meat at that. But the soul that eats only red meat is depriving itself of nourishment that comes in other ways and other forms.

Be curious, be selective, and do what really works for your own soul. Being intentional with your plan is an important step. First, decide on something about your soul that needs attention and attend to it. Then seek out a companion to walk with on the journey of transformation. This journey is always best when walked in tandem. Doing the journey alone simply sets you up for failure. A friend can encourage and speak "into" you and lead you even when you resist being led. This is more than merely being accountable to someone who will check the box if you've done it right—or wrong. Accountability alone is not enough to bring about the changes we need to make. It can help for sure. But accountability partners often settle for surface questions and quickly move on rather than stopping to look underneath the waterline of our souls and see where we're stuck and help us know why.

Making a Plan

Robert Benson said this.

> *I have noticed a curious phenomenon. One of the few things that we are reluctant to make lists about and do research about and have row of boxes to tick off about are the things that have to do with our spiritual lives. I don't know why this is.*
>
> *We say that our spiritual life is important to us. Sometimes we will even go so far as to say that it is the part of our lives that is the most important to us. We also say, at least we say about everything else that matters to us, that if we do not write it down, we will forget to do it. We say that if we are going to make sure something is done and done well, we need to make a plan so nothing gets missed and nothing gets forgotten.*
>
> *The place we are least likely to make such a plan is when it comes to our spiritual lives. We would not dream of being this way about anything else.*[2]

How do Benson's words stir inside you? Do you agree with him or not? Do you want to rip this page out, along with a few others, because they make you feel disturbed in some way? Do you want to stand up and clap? Pay attention to your soul.

Most of us resist the idea of following a plan in the care of our souls. We want to be free and spontaneous and live with grace. *Can't there be one area of life where we don't have to work, make lists, and check them twice to see who is "naughty or nice," healthy or unhealthy? And besides, just because we check the box, that doesn't mean all is "right with the world."*

This kind of reaction is understandable. I've had it myself. But I've come to believe that Robert Benson is right. For most of us, if we are really going to make progress in the care of our own souls, we need a plan. And we need to stick with it.

Consider Benjamin Franklin, one of the United States' founding fathers. He made a list of thirteen virtues and checked off how well he had done every day for many years. Franklin believed that humans were a species skilled in the art of self-deception. He believed in conducting regular self-examinations and planning ways to improve his life and open up to a relationship with God. He was able to listen to his creative soul and help write the United States Constitution, invent the lightning rod, and create a plan for the post office because he wasn't burdened with the shackles of the faults he worked to overcome. We remember Benjamin Franklin as a diplomat, politician, and scientist, but it is likely that his emphasis on self-reflection or soul care accounted for his greatness.

Measuring Progress

Whenever we're making any kind of changes to our lives, it's helpful to stop occasionally to evaluate how we're doing. Did we make the right choices? How are our new behaviors really working in our lives?

It's the same when it comes to soul care. And that's why I recommend stopping at different intervals to evaluate our own lives and experiences. Taking soul custody is a daily, weekly, monthly, and yearly responsibility.

- *Daily.* There is a dailiness to caring for our souls, and for some of us, it seems too bland to involve ourselves in our own souls' care. It may not feel powerful, glamorous, and influential enough to choose to do what is necessary to keep our souls vibrant. Sometimes we want to run and escape from our lives. But be careful to remember that escaping is not a spiritual discipline. Persistence is, however, a key to healing the violence done to our souls.

An old spiritual exercise called the Daily Examen is resurfacing again today because of the sheer practicality and benefit of asking yourself simple questions to review your day:

- What happened today that caused me to see God at work in my life and around me?
- Where did I sense the comfort and consolation of God today?
- Where did I sense the desolation in my soul today?

Questions such as these can provide good fodder for the fire to burn and sense God's presence as you examine the day you just lived. That's why it's called the Daily Examen.

Let me give you another example. Caring for my body involves making a choice about myself—my soul—multiple times a day: *Is this sandwich what I really want, or do I want to make progress in the care of my body and enjoy the body-soul connection?* Okay, I admit it. I do eat the sandwich sometimes. Also the bowl of ice cream. I'm not perfect. But remember, perfection is not the goal in the care of our souls. Life is. Life allows for messiness because the soul is messy like clay. We are seeking to become whole and holy. We are seeking to improve our relationship with God—what He intends through us. We are seeking a closer relationship with our souls.

Things happen. I make mistakes. We are often undisciplined, so we let God discipline us and turn things over to Him, asking Him to remove our defects. Tomorrow is my opportunity to make a better choice … to exercise my belief that faith without works is dead. As Abba Poemen, an old desert father, reminds us: "Every single day is a new beginning." I like that.

What individual choices are you making every day? Slow down and pause throughout each day—especially if you are stressed—and ask God to help you live out your choices. Pray "Thy will be done" and realize that you really aren't running the show. That is the humble attitude that is listening to God.

Willingness is the key to these hard, daily choices. Are we willing to take on the task of changing ourselves and taking care of our custodial souls?

- *Weekly.* Every seven days, we can take the time to evaluate: *How was my life this week? What was life-giving? What was life-draining? What would be life-*

*giving to me in the face of all of the life-draining areas
of my life?*

You may want to evaluate the state of your soul on your
Sabbath days. As you have learned, Sabbath is a time of both
looking back and anticipating the future. There is no better time
to look at our lives on a week-to-week basis. When we do this,
we can prevent sweeping issues, conflicting feelings, and competing desires from wreaking havoc through us.

- *Monthly.* Through the Potter's Inn ministry, we often
  encourage people to take a soul-care day as often
  as they can. Specifically, we encourage this to be a
  monthly activity and investment.

By taking a day a month to retreat, read, and practice some
of what we have described here, you can live in a sustainable
rhythm that will become a necessary and life-giving activity
for you.[3]

- *Annually.* Every year, the president of the United
  States offers a message called the State of the Union.
  In this message the president outlines how the
  United States is doing in its budget, employment,
  health care, international affairs, and more.

We should do something similar. Each year we should take
the time to address the state of our souls. We can then evaluate
how we are doing in areas such as body care, Sabbath-keeping,
the practice of stillness and solitude, vocations, and more. We

can enjoy the progress we have made and identify some of the areas of our lives that need more attention.

Without these "reviews" we may let up on our taking custody of our souls. Accountability and honesty leave us open to sense the flow of God's Spirit into us. We live consciously and courageously because of such honesty. We don't fear being "found out" because our lives become open and free. Soul custody requires coming to grips with the state of our souls and then choosing healthy, God-given, and God-blessed choices to regain what we have lost along the way.

A good opportunity for carrying out this annual self-examination is on a retreat. Retreats are wonderful activities that you can choose to participate in alone or with a group. I believe that as our culture continues its harried pace, we will find it even more necessary to pull away for extended times to focus—center our hearts—through extended times of untethering from the ways of the world to care for the ways of the soul.

Conclusion

The Chinese have a proverb that helps us: "The journey of a thousand miles begins with the first step." Now we must begin to take the first steps toward the long journey home to God.

Thomas Merton reminds us,

> *In the spiritual life there are no tricks and no short cuts.... One cannot begin to face the real difficulties of the life of prayer and meditation unless one is*

first perfectly content to be a beginner and really
experience oneself as one who knows little or nothing,
and has a desperate need to learn the bare rudiments.
We do not want to be beginners.[4]

The message of caring for our soul may force us to realize that we really are beginners, as much as we might want to think that our diplomas, successes, and trophies prove otherwise. Caring for our souls is an ongoing, unending discipline that we can use to make space in our lives for our souls and to make space for God. This is something I have come back to time and time again. I think you will too.

The poet Mary Oliver reminds us "there are many ways to perish or flourish." We perish every time we choose to violate our souls. Perishing does not happen in one fell swoop. Perishing happens when we neglect, violate, ignore, run on empty, fulfill roles without fulfilling our souls, and more. At our retreat, Potter's Inn at Aspen Ridge, we have a bench along the Prayer Trail that we have named the "erosion" bench. When you sit on this particular bench, you can't help but notice that the hill directly in front of you is terribly eroded. The rancher who owned this piece of land allowed his cattle to overgraze. There's no grass, yet there are deep ruts where the melting snow and rain have washed away all of the topsoil, leaving the long-lasting marks of erosion. This didn't happen in one rainstorm. It happened over years and years of neglect. This same thing can happen to our souls. But it doesn't have to. We don't have to lose our souls. We can value our souls enough to take custody of them and care for what matters most in life. We flourish when we tend to the life within us and care for it. We flourish and thrive when we give the soul what the soul requires to live.

My prayer is that you will begin to flourish most beautifully before the face of God.

> *Today I have given you the choice between life and death, between blessings and curses. Now I call on heaven and earth to witness the choice you make. Oh, that you would choose life, so that you and your descendants might live! (Deut. 30:19 NLT)*

■ ■ ■ ■ ■

Questions for Reflection

1. Read Philippians 2:12–15. What is a person's role in the caretaking of his own soul? What is God's role?

2. Spiritual disciplines or exercises are an effort on our part to "make space" for God in our lives. We do this by practicing choices that will ensure our health and spiritual vitality. Of the eight choices that we have covered in *Soul Custody,* name two or three that you feel are the most promising for your life over the course of this next year.

3. The author states, "No one gives me permission to follow Jesus and love God more than I do." What does *giving yourself permission* look like for you? When have you found yourself relying on a boss, team leader, or friend to recommend that you "take care of yourself"? What might it look like for you to do what Jesus did—practice caring for your own soul while you care for others?

4. Consider three or four of your closest friends or family members. See if you can correctly identify their learning styles and how the message of *Soul Custody* can be practiced and experienced differently. Hint: Don't forget how each one is "fearfully and wonderfully made."

5. Try to develop a twelve-month plan for caring for your soul. Take a calendar and mark certain days, times, and seasons that you want to practice trying different exercises. Consider reading the *Spiritual Discipline Handbook* by Adele Calhoun. This is an excellent resource for many other exercises that you can try, practice, and implement. Go back through each of the eight choices here and see how you can implement some of the suggested ideas. (Perhaps focusing on one choice each month could be a way to start implementing these ideas.)

Notes

1 A diagram of this illustration can be found in the appendix.
2 Robert Benson, *In Constant Prayer* (Nashville: Thomas Nelson, 2009), 78.
3 For more information on one-day Soul Care retreats, visit www.pottersinn.com.
4 Thomas Merton, *The Climate of Monastic Prayer* (Collegeville, MN: Cistercian Publications, 2005), 42–43.

Appendix

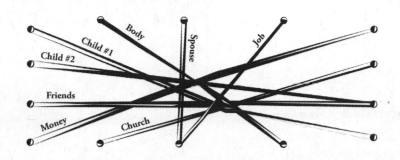

Still

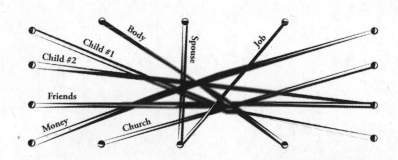

Movement

Charting the Body/Soul Connection

This exercise is meant to help you correlate your soul's wellness (identified through your emotional state) and your body's well-being. For example, someone who drinks too much alcohol might indicate that his physical and emotional well-beings were in a depressed state before or after the drinking. Yet, without spending any time putting the factors on paper, that person might never realize the interconnections. Before going to bed, create a chart with these elements. Start by writing down the foods you ate that day. Next, chart your emotional energy (body) throughout the day, showing those periods where you felt good (encouraged, bold, adventurous) as above a midline, and those times you felt discouraged, angry, and depressed as below the midline. Likewise, put your physical well-being on the grid, marking times where you felt good (strong, rested) as above the line, and marking below the line the times you felt bad (tired, achy, et cetera). Try this for a week and see if you can identify any connections between your body and soul.

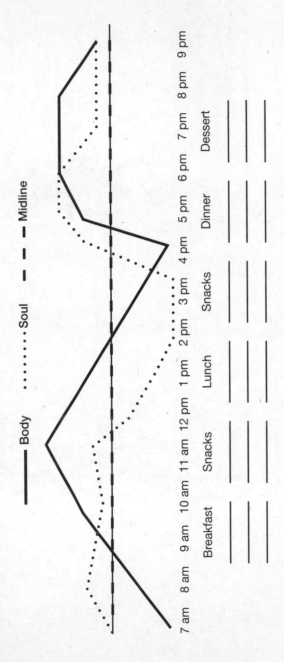

Charting the Body/Soul Connection

This exercise is meant to help you correlate your soul's wellness (identified through your emotional state) and your body's well-being. For example, someone who drinks too much alcohol might indicate that his physical and emotional well-beings were in a depressed state before or after the drinking. Yet, without spending any time putting the factors on paper, that person might never realize the interconnections. Before going to bed, create a chart with these elements. Start by writing down the foods you ate that day. Next, chart your emotional energy (body) throughout the day, showing those periods where you felt good (encouraged, bold, adventurous) as above a midline, and those times you felt discouraged, angry, and depressed as below the midline. Likewise, put your physical well-being on the grid, marking times where you felt good (strong, rested) as above the line, and marking below the line the times you felt bad (tired, achy, et cetera). Try this for a week and see if you can identify any connections between your body and soul.

——— Body   ·········· Soul   — — — Midline

7 am   8 am   9 am   10 am   11 am   12 pm   1 pm   2 pm   3 pm   4 pm   5 pm   6 pm   7 pm   8 pm   9 pm

Breakfast   Snacks   Lunch   Snacks   Dinner   Dessert

Potter's Inn is a Christian ministry founded by Stephen W. and Gwen Harding Smith, and is dedicated to the work of spiritual formation. A resource to the local church, organizations, and individuals, Potter's Inn promotes the themes of spiritual transformation to Christians on the journey of spiritual formation by offering

- guided retreats
- soul care
- books, small group guides, works of art, and other resources that
- explore spiritual transformation

Steve and Gwen travel throughout the United States and the world offering spiritual direction, soul care, and ministry to people who long for deeper intimacy with God. Steve is the author of *The Lazarus Life: Spiritual Transformation for Ordinary People*, *Embracing Soul Care: Making Space for What Matters Most*, and *Soul Shaping: A Practical Guide to Spiritual Transformation*.

Potter's Inn at ASPEN RIDGE is a thirty-five acre ranch and retreat nestled in the Colorado Rockies near Colorado Springs, Colorado. As a small, intimate retreat, Potter's Inn at Aspen Ridge is available for individual and small group retreats. "Soul Care Intensives"—guided retreats with spiritual direction—are available for leaders in the ministry and the marketplace. For more information or for a closer look at our artwork and literature, visit our Web site, www.pottersinn.com.

Or contact us at:

Potter's Inn
4050 Lee Vance View
Colorado Springs, CO 80918
Telephone: 719-264-8837

Email: resources@pottersinn.com